MW00883409

I met "the Lindas" when they trav
courses at the Theology of the Bo
are bringing what they've learned into the evangelical world. This good news
is so desperately needed in our culture, one that is so confused about the body,
sex, and marriage. *Before the Sex Talk* is a practical tool that will help equip
parents and mentors to cast a biblical vision of sex—not just the moral vision,
but the splendor of the divine story our bodies tell—that will profoundly
impact the hearts and minds of the children they influence.

Christopher West, Th.D.
President, Theology of the Body Institute
Author, *Our Bodies Tell God's Story: Discovering the Divine Plan for Love,
Sex, & Gender*

Linda & Linda paint a picture of how parents can lay out a foundation
that simplifies ongoing conversations with our children about sex. I love
how *Before the Sex Talk* illuminates the purpose of desire as a longing to live
closer to God. Linda & Linda provide conversation starters for younger and
older kids at each point along the way, some of my favorites being discussing
disappointment with our bodies, an elevated view of singleness, and the
purpose of sex within marriage. This book is not about rules but how to set an
empathetic tone for conversations about sex.

John Fort, Director of Training at BeBroken Ministries
Author of *Honest Talk*

Far too many parents needlessly fear talking with their children about sex.
In *Before the Sex Talk*, Lindas Noble and Stewart offer a refreshing and joy-
inspired framework for these most intimate conversations. They encourage
parents to approach sexual topics as opportunities to lead their children
deeper into the heart of God's love. In beautiful and holistic ways, the Lindas
share through examples, conversation prompts, and activities how children
and teens can be encouraged to understand and embrace the love for which we
are all made.

Daniel Weiss, Executive Director of the Sexual Integrity Leadership
Summit
Coauthor, *Treading Boldly Through a Pornographic World: A Field Guide for
Parents*

Few areas are more difficult than forming children's hearts and imaginations so that they grow up loving God in and through their bodies. Few books or resources provide such theologically grounded, practical advice as this one. In a world where anxiety about sexuality prevails, *Before the Sex Talk* is a beacon of clarity that will help parents become more confident in conveying the gift of God's grace through our flesh, and in the responsibilities children have to steward that gift well. This is an important and timely resource.

Matthew L. Anderson, M.Phil. and D.Phil. in Christian Ethics from Oxford University
Writer, Academic, and the Founder of Mere Orthodoxy

The Lindas get to the heart of sexual health and wholeness. Very well written with practical application. It is an excellent read and a must for every parent and person longing for the fullness of life.

Dr. Sharon May, Ph.D., LMFC
Founder and President of Safe Haven Relationship Counseling Center
Board Member, American Association of Christian Counselors

*Before the Sex Talk: A Theology of the Body Approach for Parents and Menotrs* is a true gift to a world full of people increasingly perplexed by essential questions like: Who am I? How does God view me? What is a healthy approach to sex? Amen to the fact that we finally have a practical resource adults can use to process these questions with the children who have been entrusted to them. The Lindas do an incredible job of presenting deep answers to complex questions in a way that remains approachable, achievable, and practical. We know firsthand the need for this resource. In our counseling practice we regularly see marriages and families that have been ravaged by the damaging effects of poor sexual education and understanding. This book provides a clear roadmap for us all to gain insight into healthy sexuality that is grounded in the liberating hope of the gospel. We will be recommending it often and even more importantly using it in our home with our precious children.

Matthew and Joanna Raabsmith
Executive Directors of The Raabsmith Team

You are holding "gold" in your hands. The Lindas have done a brilliant job of clearly communicating biblical truths that quite literally "change everything" in our world. Both inside and outside the church, we have heard all kinds of conflicting messages around love, relationships, singleness, sex, and marriage. Most of these messages fall dramatically short of the flourishing life God created us to experience. It can be challenging to reconcile a life of flourishing, for all ages and stages, with the confusion we have around our bodies, sex, and relationships. When we struggle as adults to understand, we feel helpless in how to communicate to our kids; therefore, the pattern of confusion continues generation after generation. My husband and I have been studying God's Word, listening to countless teachings and praying fervently for God's wisdom as we have been called to teach and write on God's design for sex. When we came across *Theology of the Body* and THE Conversation Workshop materials, we had a lot of "Aha, yes!" and "It's all beginning to make sense!" moments. The Spirit of God confirmed these truths over and over in our hearts. I could not wait to read a book with this content clearly communicated and filled with practical ways to explain these truths to kids of all ages. I now have an answer when the common question is asked: "Do you know of a good resource to help me teach my kids about sex?" Yes, yes, I sure do! I cannot wait to point people to this book! This will be a gift book to all of the dearest people in my life. I could not recommend it more! Our kids are our future and indeed, "This changes everything." Please, read this book and share it with everyone you know.

Kristin Richardson
Founder of Resurrecting Sexuality Conferences

# Before the Sex Talk

*A Theology of the Body Approach
for Parents and Mentors*

By Linda Noble and Linda Stewart

| **THE** conversation |

# Before the Sex Talk

Publisher: TCW Publishing
Managing Editor: Sarah Hauge .
Cover Design: Janet Hirata Stall
Layout: Marilee Pankratz

ISBN-13: 9798645120467
TCW Publishing
San Diego, CA

The Lindas would like to dedicate this book to those who have traveled with us and encouraged us along our long and arduous path from our first awestruck exposure to the teaching of *Theology of the Body* with Christopher West, a gifted teacher and communicator, to the many churches and groups that took a risk and invited us to make our first attempts at presenting to parents and mentors, to the participants who cheered us forward and asked great questions that helped us to clarify our message, to our families, who patiently listened to our passion for getting this message out to the church in the midst of our other responsibilities and professions, and to those who will do the hard work of investing in conversations with the kids they care so much about. In the words of so many in response to THE Conversation Workshop, "This changes everything!" May it change everything for our kids.

# Contents

# Foreword

God gives very wise thoughts to certain individuals at times I believe. I believe God gave Pope John Paul II unusual insight and inspired him to write and teach his work known as *Theology of the Body*. If this huge body of work is not clarified and explained, its impact in helping millions of individuals find greater happiness in their lives could be lost.

Linda Noble and Linda Stewart have carefully studied Pope John Paul II's work and acquired a deep understanding of it. Then, in this book, *Before the Sex Talk: A Theology of the Body Approach for Parents and Mentors*, they have taken the deep theological insights embedded therein, reached into that amazing gift of human understanding of the body, and extracted its core truths without distortion. They have then taken those core truths and interpreted them for practical application by parents and mentors. More than that, for the person who takes the time to read them, their practical explanations can be a guide to personal behavioral choices and comfort in those choices.

I only want to say a word about one groundbreaking—and I would say life-changing—concept regarding the human body, us as persons, and our sexuality that Noble and Stewart elucidate for us. They constantly point out that every individual is made in the image of God, Imago Dei, giving us fundamental dignity and value as persons. As they point out again and again, we are "embodied human persons." The body expresses the person. The body and the person are two entities, but entities that cannot be separated. Because this is true, both the body and the person now are understood in this light as precious with fundamental value.

I stated they made these concepts practical, and I would like to describe how this concept is practical. *Theology of the Body* as explained by Noble and Stewart teaches that when two people have sex they become "one flesh." Noble and Stewart highlight that this is the act of two bodies, but it means more than that. It also means that one's "person" becomes one with that sex partner. They show that for the body and person to be in sync, the embodied persons, becoming "one flesh," must be in a lifelong covenantal relationship with each other. When the body and person are "out of sync," flourishing is damaged. As they write, "What occurs in a sexual encounter that is not preceded by a covenantal promise of marriage? In that case, my voice and my body are in contradiction. To be more precise, my body speaks of lifelong union without my words providing the covenantal promise."

Noble and Stewart are groundbreakers. They have brought us concepts that we can use personally, whether single as I am (a widower) or married. These are concepts that can be life-changing as we guide those we teach and mentor to understand that sex is more than do's and don'ts, which may be the only message our young people—especially those in their twenties and still single—have ever heard.

I highly recommend this book. It is a breakthrough, and breakthroughs don't come along very often. Take advantage of it. Read it. Use it.

*Joe S. McIlhaney, Jr., M.D.*
*Founder/Chairman*
*Medical Institute*
*jmcilhaney@medinstitute.org*
*www.medinstitute.org*

# Introduction

Every parent or person working with youth longs for the children in their sphere of influence to flourish. We are all well aware that there is a conversation that is absolutely essential to that flourishing. With fear and uncertainty, we make veiled references to "the talk" with our children that looms in our future: the one about the birds and the bees, about how babies are made, about sex. We are desperate to find a compelling yet practical approach to this challenge and to discover how to have THE Conversation.

This book is an anthology of blogs written by the Lindas (coauthor team Linda Noble and Linda Stewart), the creators of THE Conversation Workshop. We hope to illuminate a worldview and provide the resources you need to help you talk differently with kids about God's design for the body, relationships, and sex. It's never too early to start this conversation and never too late to rediscover it. Parents and mentors of children from birth through adulthood will benefit from taking this journey together.

## The Source

In search of something more compelling than the sex and relationship talks we (the Lindas) heard as teenagers in youth group, and with an urgent realization as parents and educators that the typical church curriculum could do more to guide students to long-term choices that lead to a flourishing life, God directed us to a teaching called *Theology of the Body*.

This teaching originated with a hero of the faith, Pope John Paul II, and is based on 1,043 verses of Scripture. "It may well be the most in-depth biblical vision of what it means to be created male and female ever presented in Christian history."[1] It encompasses the entire biblical narrative describing God's invitation of union with himself, inscribed in the design of the human person. Rather than pairing rules related to sexuality with supporting Scriptures, this holistic approach takes the entirety of the Bible's narrative and invites us to have conversations about the body, sex, and relationships within the depths of the Story that describes God's original design, the Fall, and our ultimate destiny of union and communion with God.

Matthew Anderson—author, founder, and lead writer at
MereOrthodoxy.com—describes *Theology of the Body* this way:

> At a minimum, this account of the sexual dimensions of the
> body has a depth that our sex manuals and pastoral teachings
> have sometimes lost…This account of the body also provides
> important resources for the single and young who suffer most
> when sexuality is reduced to an animal impulse or an essential
> element of human flourishing. Exhorted to remain chaste within
> a culture that ridicules chastity as socially and biologically
> self-defeating, it's no wonder young evangelicals struggle to
> live sexually upright lives. A theology of the body patterned on
> the self-giving of the Cross, though, can begin to reframe the
> conversations surrounding sexuality and human flourishing,
> suggesting patterns of embodied life in which the single and
> married can equally partake.[2]

We recognize *Theology of the Body*'s unique vision and beauty as a
gift to the church, not just to the Catholic community. The vision and
application of *Theology of the Body* resonated profoundly with both
of our personal experiences of God and the questions and tensions
we felt in response to the other approaches to sex and relationships
that we'd encountered at church or in other contexts. We both
had individual heartfelt experiences of, "Oh wow! This changes
everything!" as we learned and continued to explore *Theology of the
Body* both together and separately.

We also recognize that one of the limitations of how conversations
about relationships and sex are typically handled in faith-based
settings is that the approach is prescriptive and rules-based, which
results in a person checking the boxes on a list of approved behaviors.
We've been deeply moved by the fact that this is not the approach
taken in *Theology of the Body*. This book and our workshops simply
offer the invitation to consider the vision of *Theology of the Body*
and the ways it differs from how these topics have traditionally
been addressed in evangelical churches. We invite you to reflect
on the ideas here and, as you do, to engage with what resonates
with you, and leave what doesn't. The main objective of each and

every conversation in this book is to invite young people "farther up and further in" (to paraphrase C.S. Lewis's words in *The Last Battle*) to a relationship with God that lovingly informs decisions about relationships and sex, not that they check each box on a one-dimensional list of rules and prescriptions.

Most of the content of our workshop, writing, and speaking is derived from the Bible, from Pope John Paul II's transformative teaching *Theology of the Body*, and from Christopher West's exposition of *Theology of the Body*. We are passionate about passing on this life-giving message to those who find themselves seeking MORE on behalf of the younger generations. We highly recommend Christopher West's book *Our Bodies Tell God's Story* as a resource for help in understanding this teaching in more depth.

### What Can You Expect From This Book?

The Lindas have been honored to be invited to speak to Christian faith audiences on the content that follows. As a result, we felt it important to create a book as a tool that provides parents and mentors a practical handle on a *Theology of the Body* approach to conversations with kids.

It is a resource for those who:

- find the teaching of *Theology of the Body* to be beautiful and compelling, and want to further explore
- have a felt need to find an approach for understanding the body, sex, and relationships that resonates more deeply than the one they personally experienced in church settings
- have tried to talk with kids on these subjects in a conventional way and felt that it fell flat
- desire to go back and rebuild the foundations for "the sex talk" and the questions that follow

We hope to provide additional resources in the future that will be of further assistance. Although we include a script that can be helpful in an approach and framework for the biological aspects of "the sex talk," we do not currently cover biology. In our workshops we work in person with adults to help them construct answers to kids' questions based on the foundations of *Theology of the Body*. We have a place on our website (https://theconversationworkshop.com/q-a) where adults can submit questions to our FAQ page. We invite you to do so as we are not able to cover the vast array of potential questions in this book.

### How To Use This Book

1. Read through the book on your own.

2. As you finish reading each chapter, review the Conversations sections, write your own answers to any questions posed, and try out the activities yourself.

3. Decide when you'd like to begin your conversations with your child or the kids you mentor and create a schedule for meeting. We'd suggest a weekly or biweekly schedule as the optimal strategy. If you prefer less structure, we still recommend that you read through the book in its entirety first in order to get a big-picture vision of where all of these topics are going and how they interconnect. Then revisit the topics in each chapter as they come up for you and those you are raising or mentoring.

4. Read through the chapter again on your own before meeting. This is for your foundational understanding of what's behind each conversation.

5. Choose at least one of the activities suggested to engage in with your child or the kids you mentor.

6. Prepare any materials that you will need for the Activities section.

7. Begin your time together using the script in the Conversations section that is most age-appropriate.

8. Engage together in the activity or activities you've chosen.

9. Find a special place to store all of the responses and creations from the Activities section and pull them out again to review previous conversations.

10. Please feel free to contact us with any questions you might have at theconversationworkshop@gmail.com.

# Chapter 1

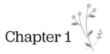

## "The Sex Talk": Where Do I Start?
### (HINT: Probably Not Where You Think)
### Linda Stewart

Parents and caregivers often want to know how or when to initiate "the sex talk." We would suggest that parents *don't* begin with "the sex talk." This might sound like a bait and switch, or as if we are avoiding the question, but honestly, the best way to deliver the topic of sex according to THE Conversation's approach is to *not* start with "the sex talk." Instead, start with the Source of each child's life.

No, not the story of where babies come from, but instead THE story of *Who* we came from—the Person each child came from. In other words, what she or he was truly born of and made for:

> You alone were created by a huddle of hearts:
>
> *Let us make human beings.*
>
> The authority of God made all of creation. But it was the *affection* of God that made all His children.
>
> The three persons of the Trinity – Father God, Jesus Christ, and Holy Spirit – gathered close together to imagine you. And God in three persons, uncontainable affections, knelt down and kissed warm life into you with the breath of His love.
>
> You are made of the dust of this earth, and you are made of the happiness of heaven, and you are flesh and you are spirit, and you are of two worlds longing for the home of forever and Him.
>
> —Ann Voskamp, *Unwrapping the Greatest Gift: A Family Celebration of Christmas*[3]

If we don't start with our true origin stories (Genesis 1 & 2, John 1:1), then a biblically-based sex talk will not be very effective.

Everything that will be covered in the following chapters, and ultimately in any conversations about sex, hinges on our children's understanding of this: Our kids were created to be in connection with Real Love, and God is the source of the Real Love they experience and give. It is impossible for our children to flourish apart from the Love of God that made us. *Our objective as parents or mentors is to communicate this truth to kids before **and** as we talk to them about the body, relationships, and sex.* When we lead with God's invitation to love others out of the overflow of his Love for us, it changes the entire tone and trajectory of any conversation about sex and relationships. Our kids need to know that the real satisfaction of their deepest desires comes from connection to God himself. Human relationships can only give us imperfect glimpses of God's Love. This realization disarms the dizzyingly frantic search for satisfaction in relationships that will ultimately disappoint.

We recommend introducing God's Love as the origin of each child's creation and the Source of real Love as early as possible (today is a great day to start!). We also recommend that you revisit this concept with your kids frequently and with a variety of approaches. The best strategy for this goes a step further than just telling kids about these ideas once or twice. It requires us to intentionally connect kids with God's Love over and over again.

How do we help children connect with God's Love?

- It begins with your own connection. In what ways do you best connect with God and his Love? This may provide clues that help children to make a connection with God.

- Watch your child or the kids you mentor with the objective of becoming an observer of who they are and what speaks to their hearts. Then, experiment with ways that you can help them connect with God. (You can do this at the earliest of ages.)

- At Christmastime, read Ann Voskamp's book *Unwrapping the Greatest Gift: A Family Celebration of Christmas* (recommended for kids around age six and older). It communicates God's Love for us in a beautiful way during Advent.

- Ask kids about their favorite ways to connect with God.

- Be mindful of what kids say about worship or nature or other experiences and comment about how you see God loving them through these things.

- Even when you can't control the environment kids are in, what are ways that you notice God reaching out and loving them? Ask kids what they see or experience from God when they are in a situation that feels out of their control.

- Look for themes that are popping up in kids' lives at any age. What messages of God's Love seem to be repeated through particular stages, or throughout their entire life?

- Be sure to initiate and engage opportunities that connect kids to God and his Love. Some examples: Be a part of a church community; consider participating in church youth camps, youth retreats, mission trips, and service opportunities; introduce art or music experiences; incorporate athletics; help kids develop friendships and relationships with young adult mentors they respect. There are endless opportunities, many of them FREE.

If you're parenting or mentoring a student who is older and resistant to these conversations, try sharing stories of connecting powerfully to God's Love from your own life. Be honest about your own journey. If you find yourself desiring to connect with God's Love in a deeper way, share this desire with your kids! Let kids know that this connection is what you want for them and for yourself. Even when kids' eyes are rolling or they aren't responding, they are listening. Try to avoid inauthentic or wordy language. Keep it simple and use language they understand. It can also be helpful to share in environments where there isn't the pressure of direct eye contact, such as in the car or while working on a project together. Use as few sentences as possible to make it easier for kids to hear you.

A practical story might be helpful here. In one of our workshops a brave and caring parent asked this question: "What if my teenager is struggling with God?" THE Conversation's answer: Be curious about the struggle. Ask questions like, *How does God feel about you? How do you feel about God? What do you believe about God that leads you to feel this way?* Many times the source of this struggle is a wounded view of who God is, who we are, and how God relates to us. By engaging in a child's faith journey with curiosity and without judgment, you can provide support in the midst of this struggle that so many (kids and adults) encounter. Listening alone, without visibly panicking, can make such a difference. Listen for perspectives or beliefs that might be causing some of the difficulty and Socratically pose genuinely curious questions in order to better understand what may be contributing to the student's struggle. Don't assume you know what they are going to say, just listen as they find the words. You don't have to have all of the answers, and if you recognize your own struggle in their words, feel free to share this. Offer that you are always available and are thankful for God's Love being a sure thing, even when we aren't sure about everything.

You can access our podcasts and blogs to help cast a new vision, or refine their vision, for God and the relationship he desires with your child. *Understanding the relationship God desires with us is where THE Conversation must start.* Before we can trust God's direction for our lives, we have to come to believe that his desire is for us to live a life that flourishes. Once we hold that belief, we are free to move forward into a discovery of his direction for our lives.

It is worth repeating: If we don't start here, with an understanding of the Love of God that created us, a biblically-informed sex talk will not be as effective. The kids in our lives will resort to seeking human relationships to satisfy their longings. And this will be reflected in their relationships and choices, regardless of how much they know about anatomy, sexually transmitted infections, and reproduction.

## CONVERSATIONS

**SCRIPTURE**

*And so we know and rely on the love God has for us. God is love. Whoever lives in love lives in God, and God in them.*
(1 John 4:16, NIV)

**YOU CAN SAY TO YOUNGER CHILDREN**

1. When we live close to God, it is the most joyful and best kind of life. We flourish.

2. When you are convinced that God loves you and wants to be close to you, it changes the way you feel about yourself and the choices you make.

3. We find God's directions for living in a close relationship to him in Scripture.

4. As you think about living close to God, how does it make you feel?

**YOU CAN TALK WITH OLDER KIDS**

1. How does God feel about you?

2. Why does he feel this way?

3. How do you feel about God?

4. What do you believe about God that causes you to feel this way?

**ACTIVITIES**

1. Create a journal with your child or the kids you mentor. Have them journal each day in the following ways:

   1) express longings

   2) list good gifts that God has given

   3) describe moments of experiencing God's Love

2. After two weeks, go back and review the journal entries together. Ask, "What are you learning about God as you journal?"

3. Consider having kids create scrapbooks with pictures and objects that represent these three categories, if they prefer that to writing.

**PRAY TOGETHER**

*"God, thank you that the Bible tells me that I was created from your Love and for your Love. Please help me to remember that your Love is the beginning and destiny of my whole life. Please help this to guide my choices and attitudes. Amen."*

# Chapter 2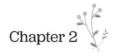

## It All Starts With A Dream
### Linda Noble

We all have hopes and dreams for our children. In fact, many of us start dreaming about their futures while our children are still growing and developing in the womb. God surprised me with our first child. I had never given much thought to children or parenting until the moment I found out I was pregnant. After my first positive pregnancy test, and after I stopped shaking, I started imagining what my child would be like. Brainstorming plans and strategies to help shape my child's life soon followed. How would my husband and I raise a child who would flourish?

As a youth pastor's wife, I had seen many young people who achieved great things, but had no passion for God or his church. I had also seen teens making choices to fully follow Jesus in spite of the cost, and in doing so leave behind the achievement of what others called success. Then there were the ones who encountered significant personal tragedies. Some of these teens' lives fell apart, but others pressed forward into intimacy with God and flourished. I observed the parents of these young people and was determined to discover the common factor among those raising children who passionately followed Jesus and experienced a full and satisfying life in spite of all the bumps, bruises, and wounding that would most certainly take place in anyone's life. After all, now I had a very personal stake in this whole parenting business.

Determining what it looks like for our children to live full and satisfying lives raises its own set of questions, though. So what does it look like for our children to flourish?

- Be good and responsible and follow all the rules?
- Be successful in school?
- Be liked by other children?
- Be attractive?
- Be talented enough to get a college scholarship?
- Be emotionally and physically healthy?
- Get married and have a family?

I think most of us would not identify any of these as a primary goal for our children, or mistakenly believe that the realization of these goals leads to flourishing. Sadly, though, I have still found myself as a parent being anxious over my child's failure to achieve them. So what is it that I'm really hoping for, dreaming of, and prioritizing?

The Wikipedia definition of flourishing includes elements that are descriptive of characteristics I fundamentally long to see developing in the lives of my kids:

- living "within an optimal range of human functioning."
- cultivating strengths, subjective well-being, "goodness, generativity, growth and resilience."
- opposite of both pathology and languishing, which are described as living a life that feels hollow and empty.[4]

Taken together, the pieces of this definition sound to me strangely like Jesus's dreams for us: "I came that they may have life, and have it abundantly" (John 10:10, NAS). The word in Greek that describes this life Jesus is talking about is not the word for biological life. The word Jesus uses refers to a beautiful, eternal kind of life that we can access here and now and, ultimately, eternally. Jesus's dream for us, and for our children, is that we experience a full and satisfying life in communion with God. He came to restore the life originally intended for us when God breathed life into the first human in the Garden of Eden.

The first man and woman were made in God's image, his glory displayed through them. St. Irenaeus describes God's dreams for us this way: "Life in man is the glory of God; the life of man is the vision of God."[5] Flourishing means living a life fully alive, fully satisfied, in full union and communion with God. We hope and dream for our children to flourish and we want them to fully experience the life that Jesus came to offer us. But how?

## CONVERSATIONS

### SCRIPTURE

*Take delight in the Lord.* (Psalm 37:4, NIV)
(For little ones: The word "delight" means joy.)

### YOU CAN TELL YOUNGER CHILDREN

1. We are created to live in a very special relationship with God. He invites you to be closer to him than you are to your mom, your dad, your sisters, your brothers, or your best friends.

2. When we live close to God, it is the most joyful and best kind of life. We flourish.

### YOU CAN TALK WITH OLDER KIDS

1. Name three things you feel you must have in order to be happy.

2. God is actually interested in you experiencing a deep, satisfying kind of happiness: one of joy and flourishing.

3. Adults, share about moments with God that brought you joy.

## ACTIVITIES

1. Go on a treasure hunt, finding gifts that God has given because he loves you (e.g. a beautiful flower in your yard, a bird, a family picture, a valued toy, your favorite snack).

2. Take pictures of things in your world that remind you that God loves you and post them on the refrigerator or a bulletin board.

3. Ask kids to share about a moment when they felt close to God. If they seem puzzled by this question, follow up by asking, "Well, can you tell me about a time when you felt sure that God loves you? Maybe it was when you were singing a worship song, maybe when you were outside listening to the birds sing, or maybe it was a time when you were listening to a Bible story." Be prepared to share an example of a moment when you personally felt loved by God in order to get the Conversation started. Plan a time during the week when you can give each child the opportunity to engage in the activity they describe.

## PRAY TOGETHER

*"God, thank you that you know what will make me joyful! Thank you that I can be joyful in you. I love you, Jesus. Amen!"*

# Chapter 3

## The Value of a Vision
### Linda Noble

Flourishing. If you were to draw or paint a picture that expresses the word "flourishing," what would you include? I (Linda Noble) don't paint or draw, but my mind is drawn to Garrapata State Park where I've gone hiking many times. Particularly after an El Nino season it becomes filled with lush wildflowers of every color, set against streams of water splashing over rocks, and towering redwood trees shading the path with greenery. In this picture I'm envisioning, I see myself there, attempting to drink it all in, enabled in the moment to be fully present.

This is the setting I imagine when I think of Adam and Eve as they experienced garden life in the beginning. But there was a precedent to even this story of beginning that has BIG meaning for us as we continue our search for how best to guide the children we care about to lives that flourish.

As we read the narrative in Genesis 1, further informed by descriptions found in John 1, we learn that God the Father, God the Son, and God the Holy Spirit existed in an eternal exchange of Love—Love poured out from one to the other, giving and receiving generative, self-giving Love. John the apostle states it simply: "God IS love" (1 John 4:8, NIV, emphasis mine).

This infinite Love overflowed into creation's beauty: the vast ocean, the exotic flowers, the towering mountains, the sun, moon, and stars, and the immense diversity of wildlife. God's culminating act of creative love was the creation of the human person. The source of our existence as human persons is the generous, generative Love of God. It is no wonder that we long for a Love that only God can satisfy.

We see Jesus conversing with a woman in John 4 who unsuccessfully sought love in disappointing human relationships. He invited her to himself as the only source of Love that would satisfy her thirst. As C.S. Lewis explains, "If I find in myself desires which nothing in this world can satisfy, the only logical explanation is that I was made for another world."[6] We flourish when we pursue what it is that we really long for, what we were made for: participation with God in his eternal exchange of Love.

This is the vision that will bring all of us life. It's easy to make the mistake of living by a set of rules if we aren't intentional about finding the way to flourishing rather than living by the default systems informed by people in the world around us. Perhaps this is the fastest and simplest route to appearing as if we're finding our way. Perhaps we're simply not sure what else to try. However, it's not sustainable. A set of rules can never satisfy that deepest longing in our hearts for the Source of Love. We must determine to do the work of teaching our children to pursue the quenching of their thirst in Jesus's Love rather than presenting them with a set of rules to live by. We must teach our children to live out of the vision of what they were made for.

This approach to life is essential to consider when it comes to having THE Conversation with the young people we care about. If we're looking for a quick and easy way to get through this uncomfortable conversation about the body, sex, and relationships with the kids in our lives, we may be tempted by a rules-based approach, but that simply won't suffice. And yet we all desire to invest in kids in a way that will give them long-term direction as they move out of the range of our control.

We must begin by reshaping THE Conversation with vision casting. We want our children to see God's design for the human person from a big-picture perspective. Once we've done this work, how does all of this vision-casting discussion help us move to our destination—a place where our children will land and make choices that will move them toward the flourishing life that Jesus is offering them? That's something we'll look at in upcoming chapters. We invite you to join us on this journey, knowing that as we travel together, our destination will become more clear. Not only that, but we really believe that along the way we will uncover the beauty and goodness of God's vision for our bodies, sex, and relationships that will irresistibly draw our children to the love and life God is inviting them to.

CONVERSATIONS

**SCRIPTURE**

*"...I have called you by name, you are mine."*
(Isaiah 43:1, NLT)

**YOU CAN TELL YOUNGER CHILDREN**

1.  Relationships with people are gifts, but they are never meant to satisfy your deepest hopes and desires. When we expect friends or family to make us happy, we will be disappointed.

2.  Your deepest desires can only be completely satisfied by being closer to Jesus than anyone else.

3.  When you are convinced that God made you and wants to be close to you, it changes the way you feel about yourself and the choices you make.

**YOU CAN TALK WITH OLDER KIDS**

1.  Talk about a time when a person disappointed you and you did not feel loved.

2.  God created you and knows exactly what makes you feel most loved. Imagine him seeing you in the midst of that disappointing moment you just talked about. What does he say to you?

3.  Pray together and ask God to make you thirsty for his Love.

**ACTIVITIES**

1. What do you like to create? Let's take some time drawing or cooking or playing with Legos. God planned to make you special, just like you make plans for your creations. What do you think God included in his plans when he was creating you?

2. Tell me about something you created that you are excited about. When God created you, he was excited. What do you think he might say as he looks at you?

3. Look up some verses that tell about the ways that God loves us. Create a card from God to you. What does he say about his love for you in this card?

**PRAY TOGETHER**

*"Jesus, thank you for loving me. You love me more than anyone else ever can—you made me! You know me and my heart. I love you, Jesus! Amen."*

**Before the Sex Talk**

# Chapter 4

## The Nagging Question: What's My Worth?

### Linda Stewart

I (Linda Stewart) want my kids to flourish. And yet in the daily waking up, packing lunches and backpacks, school, homework, carpool, extra activities, church and community living, and doing it all over the next day, I've noticed my kids can feel drained—not like they are flourishing. What seems to drain them most is when they perceive that something is threatening their personal value. They get caught up with comparing themselves to others, often in the form of what others have, such as technology, pets, or experiences. Even more ensnaring is when my girls compare themselves to their own (usually unattainable) expectations of who they should be—it starts so early! In each case, they are both assessing their personal value and searching for ways to affirm their value. Whether it's that her project should look just right or it's her expectation that she shouldn't disappoint anyone, my kids and yours are very much affected by the nagging question that plagues even adults, one most of us repeat over and over again in spite of what is accomplished, as well as at every moment of failing: "Do I have any value?"

This question, when left unacknowledged and unaddressed, can lead our kids (and ourselves) to troubling attempts to attain a temporary sense of value and worth. But when we as adults acknowledge that this is a big and ever-present question for all of us, we are able to affirm and normalize a child's search for personal value and direct him to where this question was always meant to lead: to the *Source* of his value.

*God's desire for our kids to flourish already includes the answer to this question.* He assigns a different value than the kind that our kids are used to. Typically, younger kids look to mom, dad, and other meaningful adults in their lives to be reassured that they have value. Older kids scan the people and media around them to form themselves in the image of the attractive person, the popular person, the influencer person, the good person, or the not-like-anyone-else person. Adult children who wrestle with this question may try to make themselves into the image of friends, the successful person, the desirable person, or the person who has all the answers.

Any conversation about the body, relationships, and sex depends on us communicating with our children that they don't have to make themselves into the image of any person to find value. They are made in God's image. Every child is made in Love's image, and from this Source, his or her inherent and unchanging value is established. Each child is a walking, talking, breathing image of God, and their very existence shouts, "God wanted me and so he made me, and I look like him!"

It is so crucial to spend time on the question of personal value in your conversations with kids. I sit with adults, including Christian adults, who wrestle with and grieve over questions of, "Where does my worth come from?" and "Do I have value?" Even if these adults have a biblical understanding intellectually, the concept has a hard time settling into the vulnerable space of their hearts. I often struggle with these questions myself. If these are big questions for adults to tackle, imagine the tug-of-war inside a child. What if you and I can be guides for the children in our lives so that they do not have quite the same wrestling match ahead of them? What if our conversations and our behavior toward children and each other consistently reinforces that each child's value is unchanging and uncontested because they were created in, and reflect, the image of God?

Even so, flourishing won't follow unless this conversation includes a discussion of the value of others. It is one thing for kids to know the source of their own value, but real flourishing results as they appreciate and affirm this value in others as well. When our kids can recognize the God-imparted value of each and every person they encounter, they will be living more consistently in the vision of what we were made for and what we really long for: the eternal Love of God.

We flourish when the primary focus of our lives is to be in loving relationship with God and others.

To assist you with this conversation, we want to introduce a term that is likely new to you: the personalistic norm.[7] My autocorrect doesn't even know how to handle this phrase, although it isn't new. The personalistic norm states that the person is a good toward which the only proper and adequate attitude is love. In *The Weight of Glory*, C. S. Lewis makes this applicable by saying it another way: "...it is with the awe and the circumspection proper to them, that we should conduct all of our dealings with one another, all friendships, all loves, all play, all politics. There are no *ordinary* people. You have never met a mere mortal."[8]

We can guide children to a heartfelt understanding that human value is found in these two truths: that he or she was intentionally created by God and images him in a way that only he or she can, *and* that each and every other person possesses the same value, imaging God in equally unique ways. The result of these efforts will be the very important groundwork on which the rest of THE Conversation about the body, sex, and relationships can be built.

```
┌─────────────────────────┐
│      CONVERSATIONS      │
└───────────────┐  ┌──────┘
                └──┘
```

**SCRIPTURE**

*I am fearfully and wonderfully made.* (Psalms 139:14, NIV)

**YOU CAN TELL YOUNGER CHILDREN**

1. God created you. Just like when you create or make something, it has value to you and to us as your parents. Because God created you, you have value to God. He did the best job ever when he made you. Nothing can change that. No one else in the world is just like you. You are one of a kind.

2. God also created every person you meet. Each one is valuable to him. He did the best job ever when he created each of those persons. Nothing can change that—even when you don't feel like you like _____ [your classmates, siblings, or friends], they still have value because God created them!

3. Did God make every person the same? No. God made every person special. No one else in the whole world is just like you. No one else in the whole world is like _____, _____, or _____. (Fill in the names of friends and family)

4. Every single person in the entire world was created by God and made for Love.

**YOU CAN TALK WITH OLDER KIDS**

1. What makes you special?

2. Do you ever worry that you might lose the very thing that makes you feel special?

3. How does it affect you when you are worried about losing your "special" status?

4. When God made you, he made you special in ways that reflect him. Ask God to reveal three words that he might use to describe ways that you are like him.

**ACTIVITIES**

1. Read *You Are Special* by Max Lucado.

2. Go to our downloadable conversations at theconversationworkshop.com to find a list of the ways that each child reflects the image of God. The pdf will be sent to your inbox (check in your promotions folder or spam if you don't see it soon!). Print one per child and have each child circle all the ways that he or she reflects the image of God. Print one for yourself and do it with them!

3. Try exchanging papers or print new ones and circle the ways you observe the reflection of God in each other. Have fun sharing with each other how you see God's image reflected in someone who isn't you.

4. Find a mirror. Use whiteboard markers to write words that describe the way that God sees you on your reflection.

**PRAY TOGETHER**

*"God, thank you for creating me. Thank you that I am a gift! No one else is like me. Thank you that every person I know is a gift. No one else is like them. We love you, Jesus. Amen."*

# Chapter 5

## Scripture: A Weapon, a Rubric, or a Pathway to Flourishing?

### Linda Noble

We dream that our children will flourish. And we've discovered that one aspect of a life that flourishes is to live consistently with the truth regarding human value—our own and that of others.

So let's start with the whole concept of love as an example to help us in understanding our need to find a pathway to flourishing. Loving and valuing others sounds great, doesn't it? As a mentor to children and adults, I (Linda Noble) can't imagine encouraging anything less than this. When it comes down to it, though, there is a vast array of opinions about what love actually looks like. We need to find a reliable source that will lead us to understand love better if we're going to experience a life of flourishing.

An article titled "What Love Does (And Doesn't) Look Like" in *The Huffington Post* says the following: "We must eliminate those from our lives who bring us down, and only accept those who lift us up."[9] Is this what love looks like? The Google dictionary defines love as "a feeling of deep romantic or sexual attachment to someone."[10] Is that what love is? And as we all know, there's a popular belief out there that goes like this: "You don't choose who you love." I think we're a bit confused. With all of these possible understandings of love, how do we find the best direction into a kind of life that extends authentic love and value to others? Discovering a source that we can depend on to help us love well is just one example of our need for guidance. How do we find direction for the many decisions we are required to make in life, decisions that will lead us to a life of flourishing?

God points the way to a life of flourishing, a way that includes direction for loving well, through the Scriptures. Many of us have mistakenly understood the Bible as a book of rules, a standard for performance, or a list of demands. But God's direction in Scripture is a description of the way life REALLY works for us as humans. As we grow in our confidence in his goodness and in his desire for our flourishing, the result is an eagerness to hear what he has to say about the best paths to travel in life and the ones to avoid. Moses instructs God's people Israel in the book of Deuteronomy this way:

> "So commit yourselves wholeheartedly to these words of mine. Tie them to your hands and wear them on your forehead as reminders. Teach them to your children. Talk about them when you are at home and when you are on the road, when you are going to bed and when you are getting up. Write them on the doorposts of your house and on your gates, so that as long as the sky remains above the earth, you and your children may flourish..."
> —Deuteronomy 11:18-21 (NLT)

The Psalmist writes this in Psalm 19:8 (ESV): "The precepts of the Lord are right, REJOICING the heart." I always thought this rejoicing was something that those rare people who are really holy choose obediently to do. To me, though, sometimes doing things God's way has felt more like loss. I understand now that the rejoicing comes from living life in a way that really works. When it comes to directing us into a beautiful life, who knows better than our Creator?

Jesus, hoping that the crowds would come to understand his hopes for our lives, told this story in Matthew 7:24-27 (NASB):

> "Therefore everyone who hears these words of Mine and acts on them, may be compared to a wise man who built his house on the rock. And the rain fell, and the floods came, and the winds blew and slammed against that house; and yet it did not fall, for it had been founded on the rock. Everyone who hears these words of Mine and does not act on them, will be like a foolish man who built his house on the sand.

The rain fell, and the floods came, and the winds blew and slammed against that house; and it fell—and great was its fall."

The great fall of this house doesn't come as a punishment, but as a result of choosing to build the house in a way that seems right to the builder rather than in the way that Jesus knows will keep our lives from slamming to the ground in destruction.

It's a relief to know that God isn't leaving us on our own to find a life that flourishes here and now. He isn't keeping this path to an abundant life a secret, or worse yet, hiding it from us. He has revealed it to us out of his own desire for us to live well. It's helpful to give the children we mentor this foundation for understanding the Bible: It's God's loving direction into a life of flourishing. On the basis of this foundation, our conversations with kids regarding choices they face in their teen and adult years will proceed from an understanding of a loving God who desires to direct them into a full and satisfying life. These conversations include helping our kids discover the way to REALLY love, which most likely will not line up with many of the opinions they hear from those around them. Through Scripture, they can know with certainty how to live and love in a way that leads to the best and most satisfying life possible. Who wouldn't want that?

CONVERSATIONS

### SCRIPTURE

*Direct me in the path of your commands, for there I find delight.*
(Psalm 119:35, NIV)

### YOU CAN TELL YOUNGER CHILDREN

1. In the Bible, we find direction to the beautiful life God desires for us. It makes sense that he knows the way for us to experience our very best life.

2. We can trust God's directions and follow them because we know he is leading us to the best kind of life.

3. We also learn what it looks like to love others in Scripture. When we follow God's directions found there, the result is loving actions toward others.

### YOU CAN TALK WITH OLDER KIDS

1. Why does God give us direction in the Bible for our life choices?

2. How do you feel about that?

3. Do your friends have different ideas than you about how to live a happy life?

4. Who can you trust to guide you to the best and most joyful life? Why do you think so?

**ACTIVITIES**

1. Create a map that shows a pathway through your home and ends in locating "buried treasure." Hide something that the child or children enjoy at the end of the pathway. Once each child follows the map and discovers the treasure, talk about the fact that God gives us his directions for the happiest and best kind of life in Scripture. If we follow his map, we will discover the good life that he intends for us to experience.

2. Read Psalm 119 together. Underline all the phrases that describe the good things to be found in God's Word.

3. Choose one section of Psalm 119 and pray it together, making it your own prayer.

**PRAY TOGETHER**

*"God, thank you that you created me and that you have the very best and happiest life for me—meaning life spent with you, loving you and others. Guide me to your ways and let my heart be happy to follow you. I love you. Amen."*

# Chapter 6

## Changing the Conversation About Our Bodies
### Linda Stewart

When my (Linda Stewart) girls were babies, some of my most treasured moments were when they would explore my face, arms, and hands with their tiny little hands and their expressive eyes and smiles. I would try to freeze time and capture these moments in my mind so that I could remember them later. This was before I had a cell phone with a camera, let alone a video camera, to record these beautiful interactions. Today, I can remember to some degree what it was like to have my children interact with smiles and coos as we stared at each other and their hands patted and pulled at my face or fingers. Each daughter at her earliest age was getting to know herself and me, through our bodies. Our Self is expressed through our body. It seems that babies know what the rest of us have forgotten—that the body expresses a person. *And then it changes.*

It's no wonder we forget that we are body-selves. Some of the earliest messages we receive start what can be a lifelong journey of separation and tension between ourselves and our bodies. Consider what a Common Sense Media brief says about young children and their view of the body: "Almost as soon as preschoolers complete the developmental task of mastering a concept of their bodies, they begin to express concerns about their bodies, taking their cues from peers, adults, and media around them."[11] It starts in very young children and carries on into adulthood. I hear from adult male and female clients about the strained relationships they have with their bodies and the history that created this strain. I can see this in my own life as well. An integrated view of the body-self—the idea that my body expresses my person—may be a new way of understanding and may even be uncomfortable. Some of us are used to deriving value from our bodies, and some of us are used to thinking our bodies (or what has happened to our bodies in instances of abuse or physical limitations) diminish our value. (We'll really explore that in an upcoming chapter.) But most of us are not used to considering our bodies as expressions of our person. If you and I aren't used to viewing ourselves as body-selves, then our children certainly aren't either. But we want them to inherit a different view of themselves and their bodies, right? Yes!

So, how can we impart a different view of the body? A view that is truer to what our children seemed to intuit when they were very young? We need to go back to the beginning. We need to remind ourselves of how this Story that we find ourselves in began. As parents and those who work with youth, we want to introduce children and youth to the proper context for conversations about our bodies. We've lost our way in truly understanding the relationship between body and self, but "from the beginning it was not so" (Matthew 19:8, KJV)!

Let's consider John 1:1 (KJV) to understand the beginning of our creation before going back to Genesis: "In the beginning was the Word, and the Word was with God, and the Word was God." *Theology of the Body* describes the person of God as an eternal exchange of Love: Love given, Love received, Love returned.[12] Genesis 1 and 2 tell us that our human story begins and is derived from this exchange. This creates a very important context for our creation that has meaningful implications for our kids. This is another concept we'll explore more fully in an upcoming chapter.

In an overflow of Love, God says, "Let us make man in our image, after our likeness" (Genesis 1:26, KJV). Then, in the midst of the beauty and splendor of creation, God in three persons creates the first embodied person, Adam. He is different in form and origin than any other created thing. Adam has the first body that expresses a person. And it is through his body that Adam relates to God and the animals and Eden. Not only is his the first human body (and the only body expressing his person), but we see something else unique to his creation.

"Then the Lord God formed man of the dust of the ground, and breathed into his nostrils the breath of life; and man became a living being" (Genesis 2:7, NKJV). Adam's creation, very different from any other created thing so far, encompasses what is visible and what is invisible, the material and spiritual. "The body, in fact, and it alone is capable of making visible what is invisible: the spiritual and divine."[13] Our origin story (yes, we have an origin story too, where do you think superhero stories got the inspiration?) reveals that our physical body was created with both matter and the breath of God. Our bodies this many generations later still make visible both what is physical and spiritual or unseen.

Each body expresses an unrepeatable person created out of divine Love, and each one reveals something about that Love. This is how we are known. This is how we know others. And THIS is the context in which we need to have conversations about the body with our kids. This changes the conversation about our bodies, relationships, and sex. Because now the body is no longer something we talk about apart from our person; the body expresses our person and is therefore understood in a completely different way, with completely different and life-changing implications. We will explore some of these implications over the course of the next few chapters.

For now, we invite you to experiment with the idea that we are body-selves. Find ways to model and talk with the young people in your life that acknowledge the body as an expression of who they are—the body as an expression of their person. As a marriage and family therapist, I see the value in this for children of any age. Remember the Common Sense Media brief mentioned earlier? Around preschool age, kids learn, from a variety of cues, to start viewing the body as separate from the person, something to be judged based strictly on external appearances. We want kids to instead understand that the body expresses a person, the two are connected: that what happens to my body happens to my Self, and what is happening to my Self impacts or shows up in my body. When we discuss this concept with the kids we care about, it sets a framework that informs the rest of our conversations about the body, relationships, and sex. By introducing this to a child, we are inviting him or her to a view of the body-self that is integrated.

There are lots of practical, uncomplicated ways to go about this. If a child comes to you saying he is hungry, ask questions about how he knows this. "How does your body tell you that you are hungry?" If you can tell she is tired by how she is behaving and what her body is doing, point this out using curious questions. "Do you think your body-self might be tired?" "Where do you feel tired in your body?" If she isn't aware that she is tired, she can still practice being aware of what her body is feeling and where, and how this might be connected to what her person is feeling and expressing through her body. (Adjust your questions based on the child's age and level of insight.)

For example, I know that my youngest daughter is scared or feeling vulnerable when her body-self displays particular cues. I have just begun to point this out. "I noticed that you want to be very close to me right now. I think I've picked up some clues that when you're nervous you express this by physically sticking close to me. What do you think might be making you nervous right now? Where can you feel the nervousness in your body?"

Another way to introduce the idea that we are body-selves is to remind kids that their bodies express their unrepeatable, irreplaceable, indispensable person in an unrepeatable, irreplaceable, and indispensable way. Sure, there may be doppelgangers (if the kid(s) you're talking with know what those are) and identical twins, but each person is expressed through his or her own body in a way that no person ever has been before, or ever will! Our kids need to know this, so we must remember to tell them.

I love the phrase "I see you" from the movie *Avatar*. Let kids know that you see THEM. Be curious about them. Let him know you see HIM, not his clothes or height. Let her know you see HER, not her clothes or her hair or make-up. Maintain eye contact with kids. We can put the screen, book, or project down when talking to him or her and be mindfully present with the child's body-self in front of us. This is modeling the way to "see" people.

We can also teach kids to learn to "see" people, not just bodies. Start introducing the sentence, "When I look at you, I see _____" and fill in the blank with words that describe the person, not just a physical characteristic.

CONVERSATIONS

## SCRIPTURE

*You knit me together in my mother's womb.* (Psalm 139:13, NIV) (For little ones: The phrase "knit me together" means "God made me.")

## YOU CAN TELL YOUNGER CHILDREN

1. Your body is important because it is through your body that people know all of who you are. Your body and your person cannot be separated.

2. I see you through your body. Your body reveals YOU. What does "reveal" mean? Reveal means to make known to others, or to tell. Your body TELLS who you are.

3. Could you know me if I didn't have a body? No. My body reveals me, just like your body reveals you.

4. Did you know there's someone else who has a body? He's in the Bible. Who is it? The Bible tells us that Jesus has a body. Through his body, he reveals to us what God is like.

5. Because Jesus has a body, I can see and know God.

## YOU CAN TALK WITH OLDER KIDS

1. Describe your best friend.

2. How did you learn these things about this friend?

3. Would it have been possible to really know your friend if he or she had no body?

4. What can we know about God because he came as a person, Jesus, revealed through a human body?

5. Describe a time when the appearance of someone's body caused you to fail to see the person.

6. Why is it sometimes hard to remember that you are an unrepeatable, irreplaceable, and indispensable person?

**ACTIVITIES**

1. Have a family or group discussion in which each person finishes the following sentences:

   My teary eyes reveal that I'm feeling

   _____.

   My laughing mouth reveals that I am

   _____.

   My outstretched arms reveal that I want

   _____.

   My dancing legs reveal that I am

   _____.

   My stomping feet reveal that I am

   _____.

2. Make a practice every day for a week of sharing something special that each person in the family or group has learned about someone they encountered that day.

3. Make cards for each member of the family or group that describe something unique and special about each person. Exchange cards at a special meal that you share together.

**PRAY WITH CHILDREN**

*"God, thank you for creating my whole Self. Thank you for my body. Thank you for loving me so much. Thank you that we can know you because Jesus has a body like me! I love you, Jesus. Amen."*

# Chapter 7

## Helping Kids to Integrate the Body and the Person
### Linda Stewart

I (Linda Stewart) happened to hear an incredibly insightful comment from a news anchor. It seemed to be an afterthought at the end of a story that made mention of a public figure. I honestly do not remember the overall point of the segment, but much of the focus was on this woman's clothes and accessories. Video was shown highlighting her appearance. The anchor's final comment just before cutting away to the next story was something like, "Since we don't know anything about who she is, we are left to comment on what she looks like."

This statement illustrates that we often do not realize, or perhaps we forget, that the body reveals a person. This comment also highlights, rather profoundly, the way we engage with each other: We have a tendency to separate the body from the person.

The previous chapter explored the truth that the body expresses a person. One of the greatest implications of that truth is that the body and the person can't be separated. But we attempt to do this all the time, and this particular news anchor came to the realization on air that since she didn't know a particular woman's *person*, she was limited to commenting on what this particular woman's *body* was wearing. Every woman's and every man's body expresses her or his person, and we can't escape the ramifications of ignoring this truth. We limit ourselves and cause harm to others when we diminish another person solely to a physical body.

The moment you or I separate a person from his or her body, it becomes easier to value or judge that person. It becomes possible to use that person as an object. When I view my body as separate from my Self, I begin to see my body's appearance as a source of my value. I can begin to choose to use my own body as a tool when it suits me. Any time that I attempt to view my own or another's body as separate from the person, I am moving away from a life that flourishes and toward a life that fails to see people as God sees them.

Since our children learn from adults, we see and hear children separating persons from bodies quite frequently. Verbal judgment based on appearances means seeing another as strictly material. There's even a term for this: "eye candy." Okay, so young people don't use the words "eye candy" anymore, but they do tend to reduce themselves and others, all of whom image God in an irreplaceable and unrepeatable way, to mere objects for personal consumption.

Not only does this practice impact the ways our kids see and treat others, but it also impacts the ways they see and treat themselves and their own bodies. Does your son view himself as separate from his body? Does your daughter view or judge her person and her body separately? If so, which is she harder on? Which does he give more attention to?

We can really help our children by acting as mirrors that serve to consistently reflect back to our kids that they are body-selves and that the person cannot be separated from the body. When we intentionally diminish this habit of separation, it changes our conversations about the body, relationships, and sex. We can raise and mentor kids to habitually seek to see each person, expressed through his or her body. We can influence kids to see that regardless of the situation, his or her person is impacted by what his or her body is doing. We can offer young people a picture of what it means to live as an integrated body-self so that they can choose to do with their bodies that which is consistent with their person—in other words, they can be empowered to make choices with their bodies that affirm the fact that they are a person imaging God in a one-of-a-kind way. She was made from divine Love and when connected with that Love, overflows with love of God and others.

I don't have all of this down in raising my two girls. I am trying to keep up just like you are. My efforts go well one minute and often blow up the next. Even so, I attempt to affirm that the body and the person can't be separated with conversations related to the experiences my kids already encounter. For instance, they know that I don't like "body songs." My definition of a "body song" is any song where the singer croons about someone's body and doesn't include lyrics extolling the *person*. My girls sarcastically say, "Oh Mom, here's your favorite song!" And we talk through why, including how offensive and hurtful it is to have someone separate our body from our person. My kids eventually ask me to change the song so they can be free of the "teachable moment." The conversation continues as I "enlighten" them about the ways that the body belonging to the person referred to in the song is being described in a very selfish manner. I put effort into communicating the importance of seeing others as persons, not as bodies that can be discussed casually or possessively.

Let's go back to the news anchor referenced before. As you watch TV or movies with children up through teenagers, listen to music, or read with them, don't hesitate to point out examples of the separation of body and person. Be encouraging as you challenge kids to think about these issues. Ask questions like, "Well, what can we know about how this person reflects God through her body-self?" "Is he reflecting joy through his smiling face and laughter?" "She is showing strength and protection like God by standing up for her sister and walking with her away from bullying." Even if we don't know anything about a person, we can take a position of curiosity and awe knowing that this person, imaging God through this body, is a wonder that has never before been on this earth.

If you'd like a book and movie suggestion along these lines, consider the *Wonder* book series by R. J. Palacio and the movie *Wonder*, based on the book. These books and movie are beautifully done and encourage the reader to seek to know the person who is expressed through the body, including those whose appearance is different or unexpected in some way. Read and preview first to determine if these are appropriate for the children in your life.

```
         ┌──────────────────────────┐
         │      CONVERSATIONS       │
         └──────────────────┐   ┌───┘
                            V
```

**SCRIPTURE**

*Dear friends, let us love one another, for love comes from God.* (1 John 4:7, NIV)

**YOU CAN TELL YOUNGER CHILDREN**

1.  Your body and your person cannot be separated. Just like macaroni and cheese or hide and seek, they go together. You can't take them apart. Can you think of other things that go together or that can't be separated?

2.  Any living person's body you see, whether someone else's or your own, is never, ever only a body. God is inviting us to love—to see others not just as a body but as a "somebody."

3.  Any choice you make affects your WHOLE Self, not just your body—because the body and the person cannot be separated. We are body-selves. When you choose to show love with your body to a friend or family member, how does that make you feel inside?

**YOU CAN TALK WITH OLDER KIDS**

1.  Can you give me some examples of music lyrics that describe a person's body without any curiosity about who that person really is?

2.  It might feel great at first to be complimented on your body, but how do you think it might feel if your best friend *only* seemed to notice your body? Why would it feel this way?

3.  When you make a poor choice, how does that feel in your body? When you make a great choice, how does that feel in your body?

## ACTIVITIES

1. Create a poster outlining each child's body. At the top, write "God created my whole Self!" Ask each child to write answers to these questions about themselves inside the outline:

   What do you hope for?

   What are you afraid of?

   What are your favorite things?

   What are some words that describe your personality?

2. Read *If Only I Had a Green Nose* by Max Lucado.[14]

   Ask children what was most important to the Wemmicks in the town.

   Did the other Wemmicks get to know Punchinello? Why not?

   How does it feel in your body when others are only interested in the way you look?

3. Plan a family or group activity that gives your family or group joy. This could be swimming at the lake, listening to music, dancing, or cooking a meal together.

   Talk about each one's favorite moment during the activity.

   Ask each member of your family or group what joy feels like.

   Make the point that we experience joy in our bodies because we are whole persons.

## PRAY TOGETHER

*"God, thank you for creating my whole Self. Help me to see myself and others as whole persons and not just as bodies. Please fill my whole Self with your love. Amen."*

# Chapter 8

## Kids Judge Their Bodies: How You can Help
### Linda Stewart

On some level, we're all aware that the culture we live in has taught us to judge our bodies. This habit of judging bodies influences a huge number of our choices, creating impediments that keep us from lives of flourishing. How can we stand in the way of this onslaught and replace the damaging thoughts that shape our kids' self-assessments?

In previous chapters, we've established that we are embodied human persons, that the body expresses the person, and that the body and the person can't be separated. It's now important to integrate the value of the person with the way we view the appearance of the body. The related question is this: How is the value of my person related to the way I see my body?

The perceived answer quickly becomes a personal one, so I'll (Linda Stewart) just write from my own experience. I could give a good Sunday school answer: "If I had a God-made price tag attached to my person, it would read, 'PRICELESS.'" Admittedly, it's easier for me to say this about others. With an internal struggle that would be invisible to you, I could agree that I am priceless because God sees me as priceless. But on a deep level, conceding that this God-made "priceless" tag could accurately be attached to my own body is more likely to make me cringe. I evaluate my body with a different kind of criteria than I use when thinking of others. Despite the value God claims he's bestowed on me, I sometimes give my own evaluation of my body more weight than God's. On top of that, my husband and I have occasionally started exchanging comments (when we are sure the kids aren't around) about our aging bodies. Once aging is thrown into the mix, the number of days that I assign a positive value to my own body, and therefore my body-self, drastically reduces.

It's not just me. Our Western culture tends to encourage us to sculpt and enhance the appearance of our bodies in an attempt to feel better about ourselves and get others to notice and affirm us. But our bodies have value WAY beyond how they measure up to cultural standards of beauty. Our bodies are God's design for expressing our person made in the image of God. Each embodied person images God in an irreplaceable and unrepeatable way. The truth is that since I am a body-person, and my body and my person are inseparable, my body must also be judged as priceless (both by myself and by others). My body expresses the beauty of my person as a reflection of God.

THIS truth is a gift we can give our kids and the kids we work with. Together, we can help our kids to reframe messages they've absorbed, or prevent them from even starting to internalize the message that the body's appearance is a source of our value and worth. What are some practical ways to do this?

The most effective way is probably the most difficult because it requires that we as parents, grandparents, and mentors deconstruct our own beliefs that affirm the body as a source of our value. However, if we make the effort to model the truth for kids, it can be transformative. Research across cultures repeats many times over that children learn what is modeled to them by their caregivers. Through our relationships, we can demonstrate that every body is priceless because it expresses the irreplaceable and unrepeatable beauty of that person as a reflection of God. We can model this same truth through how we treat our own bodies as well as the bodies of others.

The other day my daughter remarked, "Mom, you never say anything about people being fat or skinny. You don't talk about how people look. You don't talk about us that way either." This for me was a moment of, "Yay! The experiment is working!" It reminded me to stay the course. I celebrate that she noticed enough to say something. It was also a reminder to be more consistent, because if I'm being honest, I am intentional about this around my kids, but it isn't always the way I communicate about my own body when I'm talking with my husband or adult friends with no children around. This is an ongoing process, and we do make mistakes, but I have seen enough payoffs that I know it's worth continuing down this path, being consistent not just in order to model behavior to children, but also to develop the practice of viewing my body-self as God intends. I intentionally refuse to assign value based on physical appearance— the appearance of others or my own.

Recently, I came across a phenomenal article called "Shame-faced"[15] by Dr. Dan Allender that gave some direction for making the shift in the way we judge bodies. Dr. Allender shares in the article that he experienced many childhood wounds surrounding the appearance of his nose. These wounds shaped the way he judged his own body and resulted in shame. He encountered God's healing through a conversation with his granddaughter, Elsa:

> She looked again in my eyes. This time she put her hand on my nose and said, "Papa, I love your big nose." She slipped her arm around me and gave me a child's version of a bear hug. That night as I prayed before falling into a languid sleep, I heard Jesus ask me: "Will you let me touch your nose? Will you let me bless your face like Elsa?"[16]

What if we could touch the parts of our bodies that influence the way we judge our own value? What if we allowed Jesus to bless them? What if we could help our children to do the same?

Another practical approach to affirming the body's value is to affirm the body as an *expression* of who we are, rather than as an acceptable or unacceptable (an evaluation we all know can sometimes depend on the day) *accessory* to who we are. Some examples here:

- When a child comments about her body's appearance, bring the conversation back to the ways her body expresses her person. One example from my experience is the story of a teen who expressed serious concern over scarring from a surgical procedure. While really listening to this teen and hearing his experience, I offered a different perspective that brought the conversation back to a focus on the whole embodied person: "Just think of all the scars and marks that your body collects over the course of your lifetime," I said to him. "One of the ways your body expresses who you are is by keeping track of some of the experiences along the way that make you, you."

- Any time you receive an innocent comment from a young child about the size or shape of your legs, any scars, shape of your tummy, or even the skin hanging on your arms (please tell me I'm not the only one!), address your response to the body part mentioned and connect it with the way that part expresses something about you: "No one else in the whole world has my arms. My arms carried you when you were little, they hold you when you're sick, and they tickle you when you ask me to. My arms help me to express my love for you and others." "No one else in the whole world has my tummy. My tummy digests my food so that I have good energy for work or play each day." "No one else in the whole world has my legs. My legs let me run when we play and are strong to explore with you. Sometimes when you're tired my legs help me love you well and do the walking for both of us when I carry you."

- If you have or work with older kids, make different connections. Gently but consistently challenge statements your teen makes about her body as the source of her value. Affirm your teen's body as an unrepeatable and irreplaceable expression of who she is in those moments that she draws value from her appearance. For example: "When I look at your body, I see the beauty of your smile that makes people feel comfortable and loved!"

When we assign value based on appearance, we also are unintentionally separating the body from the person, which causes harm to the other person and to ourselves. It is a detour on the path to flourishing and impedes our participation in and experience of the eternal Love of God we were made to receive. When I assign myself value or try to prove my value to others based on my bodily appearance, I am attempting to use my body to validate myself.

I harm myself when I fail to acknowledge my body-self as an irreplaceable and unrepeatable embodied image of God. Instead, I can choose to live out of the confidence that comes when I acknowledge the truth I'm often tempted to reject.

We hope for our kids to see themselves and others as whole embodied persons of inestimable value and worth. They are inundated with messages conveying the opposite: that value and worth are judged solely on the body's appearance or ability. Instead of inadvertently and unintentionally affirming this damaging message, let's work together to make sure kids understand that the body's appearance is an unrepeatable and irreplaceable expression of who we are as human persons made in God's image. Let's cast a bigger and more beautiful vision for the body.

CONVERSATIONS

**SCRIPTURE**

> *So God created man in His own image; in the image of God He created him; male and female He created them.* (Genesis 1:27, NKJV)

(Explain: When it says God created man in his own image, it means he created every person, male and female, in his own image.)

**YOU CAN TELL YOUNGER CHILDREN**

1. Your worth—the value of who you are—is not increased or decreased by your appearance or physical abilities (in other words, what you look like or anything you can or can't do).

2. The Fall that happened in the Garden of Eden made it harder for us to see ourselves and others clearly. The Fall made it just as challenging for us to see and remember that we are unrepeatable and irreplaceable. It's like we're looking at ourselves and one another through foggy glasses.

3. Jesus came to free us from our brokenness and invites us to live a new kind of life with him. He makes it possible to see others and ourselves as he sees us.

**YOU CAN TALK WITH OLDER KIDS**

1. What are your thoughts when you look in the mirror each morning?

2. What does God say about the person you see in the mirror?

3. Are there parts of your body you find difficult to see in a positive way? If so, how does that affect your choices or how you think of yourself? How does that affect your relationships with others?

4. What do you think Jesus wants to say to you about these parts of your body?

**ACTIVITIES**

1. Take some pictures of your child or the kids you mentor and print them out. Pray with each child over each part of his or her body, especially those that they have complained about, and ask Jesus to bless these parts.

2. Wrap these pictures up in a gift box and place it in an accessible spot. Whenever the child makes a negative comment about his or her body, grab the box and ask what's in it. Remind the child that his or her body reveals an irreplaceable, unrepeatable, and indispensable person loved by Jesus.

3. Play a game that challenges each member of the family or group to think about the ways each part of our body enables us to be a gift that expresses Jesus's Love to others.

**PRAY TOGETHER**

*"God, thank you for choosing to make me and everyone else in a way that shows off some of what you are like. Thank you that my whole body-self images you in an unrepeatable and irreplaceable way. Amen."*

# Chapter 9

## Why Male and Female? God, What Were You Thinking?

### Linda Noble

*What were you thinking?* I (Linda Noble) have posed this question many times: when my then five-year-old daughter decided to run up on the stage and stand next to the pastor as he delivered his message, when my son decided as a young adult that it was a great idea to practice front flips off a beachside bluff, or when my husband decided to teach the cat to drink water from a glass on the kitchen counter. We all have moments when we step back and wonder incredulously what was going on in the mind of another when...!

We've been on a journey together with *Theology of the Body* and the work we've done in creating a tool based on *TOB* for those mentoring kids. In the beginning, God created us in his image and invited us to a life of flourishing in communion with himself. In his original design, we were created as embodied persons. Our bodies are good and it's only through them that we can be known by and engage with others. As we relate to one another, we cannot separate the body from the person without inflicting wounds or alienation. Our bodies are not accessories that add to or take away from our ultimate value as persons. Having grasped all of this, we may stop and wonder, "Then why, O God, did you make us humans with male and female parts? What were you thinking?"

**Possible answers have included:**

- To add a little excitement to life!
- For the enjoyment of sexual relationships.

- To propagate the human race.
- To establish families.
- To build character from the conflict that ensues.

Let's go back once again to Genesis to discern God's purposes. In Genesis 2:23 (KJV) we find Adam's response to this new "Eve" person who has arrived on the scene: "This is now bone of my bones, and flesh of my flesh." Adam realizes that he is now joined in creation by another embodied person. Before this moment, he has encountered a multiplicity of other creatures, but none made in the image of God, expressed in flesh. Eve is the same, yet different. Together, as persons who may enter into union and communion with one another as well as with their Trinitarian Creator, male and female reflect God's image more perfectly. As *Theology of the Body* says, "Man becomes the image of God, not so much in the moment of solitude as in the moment of communion."[17]

Notice that Adam's excited exclamation in Genesis 2:22 is a response to his discovery of another embodied person. When I was a young person, listening in rapt attention to a highly-anticipated sex and dating talk in youth group, there seemed to be a consensus that Adam was MOST enthusiastic about the appearance of a gorgeous body with whom he could now have sex! But that, I have come to realize, is a description of lust, and lust had not yet entered this pre-Fall picture. Because of this we know that Adam only wanted, with the Love of God he had experienced, to love Eve as another person expressed through her body. She was invited into the eternal exchange of love flowing between these two persons made in God's image and the Godhead.

We should also take note of the biological differences in the creation of male and female. Our biological designs enable male and female to join in the most intimate union and communion possible for two embodied persons. The result of this union, experienced consistently with God's design, is life-giving love, a reflection of the Love of the Trinity that resulted in the abundance of life in creation. The anatomies of male and female bodies reveal that we are made for union, communion, and generative love.

Awareness of the design of male and female anatomy should lead us not to the conclusions that we were all made to have sex, that we were all made to generate babies, or even that we were all made for human marriage. Rather, our bodies are a visible sign of life-giving Love so that "Every man is called in some way to be both a husband (self-gift) and a father (fruitfulness). Every woman is called in some way to be both a wife (self-gift) and a mother (fruitfulness)."[18]

A beautiful picture of this vision for the human person can be found in C.S. Lewis's *The Great Divorce* as he recounts the story of the Woman of Great Love. The narrator of this story travels to heaven and, accompanied by a Spirit guide, explores the deep truths that become visible in this place. The narrator refers to the Woman in saying, "But I have forgotten. And only partly do I remember the unbearable beauty of her face."[19] He inquires as to the identity of this woman and this is what he learns:

> Her name was Sarah Smith and she lived at Golders Green... Every young man or boy that met her became her son—even if it was only the boy that brought the meat to her back door. Every girl that met her was her daughter...Every beast and bird that came near her had its place in her love. In her they became themselves. And now the abundance of life she has in Christ from the Father flows over into them.[20]

THIS is what God was envisioning when he created male and female in those first days of creation. The picture of male and female imaging God's invitation to life-giving love and communion is beautiful and inclusive, and yet stands in stark contrast to all that most of us have learned. Could we possibly find a new way to teach our own children God's design for our creation as male and female?

CONVERSATIONS

**SCRIPTURE**

*Adam and his wife were both naked, and they felt no shame.* (Genesis 2:25, NIV)

**YOU CAN TELL YOUNGER CHILDREN**

1.  God created men and women in the very beginning.

2.  He hoped that they would love one another in the same way that he loved them.

3.  When we stay close to God and feel loved by him, we are able to love one another with his Love.

**YOU CAN TALK WITH OLDER KIDS**

1.  When we see that God created male and female persons it is a picture that reminds us that we are invited by God into a relationship of love and togetherness with him.

2.  Our creation as male and female is a picture that points us to some small understanding of the Love flowing from the persons of the Trinity that generated life in the moment of Creation. When we love others well, how does it affect their lives?

3.  Our bodies are signs of self-giving love. They remind us that we are invited to join God in love-giving and life-giving throughout all of the seasons of our lives.

    Describe some of the ways that God loves us. How can we imitate God's kind of love as we love others? For example, God creates beautiful things, like flowers, for us to enjoy. We can share a gift of flowers with someone.

**ACTIVITIES**

1. Make a poster with words and illustrations that describe God's Love for us.
2. Talk about ways that we can love others with God's kind of Love.
3. Plan a project for this week. This project should give kids the opportunity to love someone else with God's kind of Love.

**PRAY WITH CHILDREN**

*"Thank you, God, that your Love is so big. Thank you for giving us clues about your Love by creating us with bodies that are able to give and receive love. Please help me to fill up with your Love so that I can love other people well. Amen."*

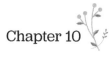

# Chapter 10

## The Fate of Marriage
### Linda Noble

Growing up in the San Francisco Bay area in the 1970s, I (Linda Noble) became keenly aware of the emerging protest against the institution of marriage, which could be boiled down to this line: "Marriage is just a piece of paper!" That protest was not merely evidence of a fleeting trend, and decades later these issues are just as deserving of our further exploration. In the 2010 *Time* magazine article "Who Needs Marriage: A Changing Institution," Belinda Luscombe writes, "When an institution so central to human experience suddenly changes shape in the space of a generation or two, it's worth trying to figure out why."[21] That's what a Pew Research Center poll in 2010 attempted to do, ultimately reaching this conclusion that is also referenced in the *Time* article:

> What we found is that marriage, whatever its social, spiritual or symbolic appeal, is in purely practical terms just not as necessary as it used to be. Neither men or women need to be married to have sex or companionship or professional success or respect or even children.[22]

Results of the 2012 US Census reveal that two-thirds of couples married that year had shared a home together for more than two years prior to marriage.[23] If our understanding of marriage is reduced to it being no more than a necessary part of a happy life, none of this will feel like a surprise. But what if there is more to it?

The following is just a sampling of the scripts our kids will hear repeated over and over in the world they encounter:

- Sex has very little to do with marriage and weddings.
- Sex as a dating practice hurts no one as long as it is consensual.
- Loving someone gives us the right to sex with him or her when it's consensual.
- Celibacy is a cruel and unusual punishment.
- Sex is an essential ingredient for happiness.
- Marriage is unnecessary and optional.
- Monogamy is largely unrealistic.
- Be with the one you love no matter the cost.
- Marriage is an institution that simply has little meaning for us today.
- A wedding is the ultimate party and the culmination of all of our dreams.
- The marriage ceremony is merely the precursor to the wedding celebration.

Although it can be tempting to respond to all of the above with a furrowed brow and head shaking, I wonder if a large part of the responsibility for this fog that surrounds marriage and sex lies with us as Christ-followers. For many years, many of us who identify with that label have relied on "the rules" to guide young people in the direction of marriage. Those of us who had the advantage of growing up in youth groups will recall the Bible verses that instruct us to avoid having sex outside of marriage. These plainly-stated rules gave us boundaries for living. Church leaders and parents have asked our teens to wait for sex until marriage by challenging them to sign pledge cards and wear purity rings. We've had good intentions, but in talking with teens in these limited terms we've crippled our ability to cast a vision for God's intended meaning of sex, marriage, and weddings.

I, probably like many of you reading, grew up in church youth groups, where I was given the choice to obey "the rules" (or not) but was unable to give compelling answers to emerging questions surrounding the "why" and "what for" of marriage. This failure, in spite of the nurturing and education I received in church culture, was due to my rules-based, visionless understanding of these topics. As an adult I found myself virtually helpless to guide others beyond passing on what was given to me, and I discovered that I also didn't have what I needed to sustain life-giving choices of my own.

How do we find our way out of the fog so that we can help our kids catch a vision of truth more profound and compelling than "the rules"? We have to begin by admitting that "the rules" have failed us. We have depended on them for our instruction rather than searching for and communicating the meaning behind God's design for marriage.

We'll start with a rather surprising statement made by Jesus in Matthew 22:29-30. The Sadducees, who taught that there is no resurrection, were stalking Jesus one day and thought they might stump him with a question about the fate of a woman who died after surviving seven deceased husbands with no children(!). Their ridiculous question reveals the reality of their hidden agenda: "In the resurrection, therefore, whose wife of the seven will she be?" (Matthew 22:28, NASB). Jesus's answer: "You are mistaken, not understanding the Scriptures nor the power of God. For in the resurrection, they neither marry nor are given in marriage" (Matthew 22:29-30, NASB).

What? No marriage in heaven? That means no sex or romance in heaven either?? If we're honest, even Christ-followers have been so influenced by culture that we've bought into the idea that finding "the one," or sexual experiences, or a Christ-centered marriage, or some combination of those things, is prerequisite for a satisfying and full life. In fact, we may not be aware we've made these assumptions, but when we or our friends find ourselves in a state of singleness, we urgently seek to remedy the situation with an immediate search for a new partner.

If it's true that life isn't meaningful and fulfilling apart from sex or marriage, then how is it possible for eternity in heaven to be a place of abundant and flourishing life when there won't be marriage there? The Message version of this conversation in the book of Matthew goes like this: "Jesus answered...At the resurrection we're beyond marriage. As with the angels, all our ecstasies and intimacies then will be with God" (Matthew 22:30, MSG).

Maybe we need to rethink. Maybe the essence of what we're really longing for during the earthly trek of our lives is something MORE than earthly marriage. Maybe, as we suggested earlier, our primary calling is to find the satisfaction of all our desires by immersing ourselves in God's Love, and then to love one another from the overflow of God's Love. Marriage or being in a romantic relationship seem far less important when we think about our life's purpose this way.

If that's all the case, why get married at all? We can find one answer in the New Testament. In Ephesians 5:31-32 (NIV), the apostle Paul describes marriage as a picture of the relationship God is inviting us to: "For this reason a man will leave his father and mother and be united to his wife, and the two will become one flesh. This is a profound mystery—but I am talking about Christ and the church." Throughout the Bible we see similar teachings: that the primary descriptor of a relationship with God is that of a husband to his wife. The marital relationship, it seems, is a map intended to point the way for us to better comprehend deeper truths about God, ourselves, and his invitation to union and communion with himself. The marriage relationship is the context in which we learn to image God's self-giving, sacrificial Love. This thought lays the groundwork for an understanding of marriage that has far-reaching implications we'll continue to explore in the following chapters.

## CONVERSATIONS

**SCRIPTURE**

*Jesus answered… "At the resurrection we're beyond marriage. As with the angels, all our ecstasies and intimacies then will be with God."* (Matthew 22:30, MSG)

**YOU CAN TELL YOUNGER CHILDREN**

1. When we expect friends, marriage, or family to make us happy, we will be disappointed. People can never love us as well as God does.

2. Our deepest longing is to be loved by Jesus even though sometimes it feels like all that we need is to be loved by people.

3. Marriage is a picture that God created to show us what his Love looks like. When you look at the way married people love each other, what do you see that reminds you of the ways God loves us?

**YOU CAN TALK WITH OLDER KIDS**

1. God created marriage to show us what it looks like to be loved by him.

2. In what ways do you notice husbands and wives loving like God does?

3. What are some ways we expect our friends to meet our needs?

4. In what ways do you think our relationships with our friends and family might change if we felt so loved by God that we were able to enjoy our friendships with fewer expectations?

**ACTIVITIES**

1. In a journal, list ten things your best friends do for you that make you happy.

2. Under each entry, write a prayer: "Thank you God for showing me the way that you love through my friend _____."

3. In your journal, write a list of ways that God shows his Love to us.

4. At dinnertime or before bed each night this week, ask each member of the family or group to share or think about one gift of Love that Jesus gave him or her during that day.

5. Find some family wedding pictures. Ask kids to talk about what they notice about the pictures. Talk about how a wedding is a picture of God's Love for us.

**PRAY TOGETHER**

*"God, thank you so much that you have given me a heart that wants more. Please help me to understand and look for what my heart really longs for. Please grow my heart's love for you. Help me to recognize and live out your love in other relationships! Amen."*

# Chapter 11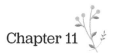

## The Bachelor and Porn: The Truth They Reveal About Romance, Sex, and Marriage
### Linda Noble

So what is up with *The Bachelor* and *The Bachelorette*? I (Linda Noble) have to confess that I really don't get the appeal. However, I frequently overhear excited interchanges regarding these shows. People are obsessed with them. I find that I have to back away slowly in order to avoid alienating friends and family members with my own impassioned speech. After some quiet reflection, I've realized what I actually need to do is take a breath and ask the deeper questions lying here: *Why have these shows drawn top ratings for the past sixteen years? What can I learn as I observe friends and family who seem inextricably drawn to the stories revealed during these episodes?*

In a *Time* magazine article from March 4, 2018, Samantha Cooney posits a possibility: romance. "Millions are still riveted by a show characterized by its extravagant dates, abundance of champagne and end goal of getting engaged by the season finale."[24] Amy Kaufmann, another writer for *Time*, is quoted in the same article: "I think why we're so obsessed with the show has something to do with our desire to have fantasy and romance in our life!"[25] If this is the source of the appeal, is that a problem? I think it is. The vast majority of us will never experience this level of romance and even if we do, it's definitely not sustainable.

How, then, can we possibly be satisfied with relationships that fall short? As a culture writer for *The Huffington Post* comments in a 2017 article, "It magnifies and enacts the sort of reductive tropes and expectations we face in the real world, especially the real dating world."[26] All of this points to one conclusion: In spite of the stark reality of the inadequacy of romance and marriage as a means to a fulfilling and satisfying life, the undeniable attraction to stories of romance and love persists.

I imagine that some readers will not resonate with this prevalent longing for romance, love, and marriage. Sometimes our life experiences or our woundedness channel our desires in a different direction, and for some people that direction is pornography. Recently I read the following in an article sourced from an organization named Fight the New Drug: "Porn sites received more website traffic in 2020 than Twitter, Instagram, Netflix, Zoom, Pinterest and LinkedIn combined."[27] As I continued down the web page, reference was then made to some thought-provoking Twitter posts on the subject:

- Porn doesn't play games, porn doesn't text back slow, porn gives you exactly what you ask. I love porn.
- I love the happy endings in porn.

These are just two of the many tweets describing a love for porn. If we set aside judgment regarding the morality of porn for a moment, we realize that it exposes human longings and desires closely related to those experienced by viewers of *The Bachelor*: the longing to grasp the illusion of a relationship that provides connection and happy endings.

In his book *The Denial of Death*, Ernest Becker writes, "We live in an age of apocalyptic romance. We've removed God and his design for marriage and replaced him with unbearable expectations for transcendent relationships."[28] There's no denying that we are relational beings. Every human person has expectations and hopes that if we do things right, our connections with other persons will somehow fill a deep void. These longings and desires have been misdirected, whether in a quest for romance or a thirst for porn or some other way to satisfy our need for what only an intimate relationship with God can provide. It's important to take an honest look at the disappointments we experience in our relationships and ask ourselves what it is that we are searching for. However our longings or desires are misdirected, the results are similar: We crush and destroy the deeper connection we are seeking.

The word "apocalyptic" comes to mind here. It can be defined in terms of a catastrophic ending, but I'd like to look at the meaning in Merriam-Webster's: "wildly unrestrained," "grandiose," or "climactic."[29] Thinking back to our conversation on marriage in the previous chapter, we saw that Jesus addressed the religious leaders' erroneous thoughts regarding marriage when he said, "You are mistaken, not knowing the Scriptures nor the power of God. For in the resurrection, they neither marry nor are given in marriage" (Matthew 22:29-30, NKJV). In the resurrection—or in other words, in the eternal kind of life—earthly marriage will be absent. Why? Because in that place, we truly will experience an apocalyptic romance, one in which all barriers between God and us are removed and we are finally and completely one with him. (See Ephesians 5:31-32, and many others.)

In fact, we are invited to taste of this other kind of relationship even now. C.S. Lewis describes it this way:

> It would seem that Our Lord finds our desires not too strong but too weak. We are half-hearted creatures, fooling about with drink and sex and ambition when infinite joy is offered us, like an ignorant child who wants to go on making mud pies in a slum because he cannot imagine what is meant by the offer of a holiday at sea. We are far too easily pleased.[30]

As John Piper clarifies in his 2013 article "We Are Far Too Easily Pleased," "Lewis says, No, your desires aren't the problem. The weakness of your desires are the problem..... In other words, your desires for the great things that God is offering you are way too small. Your problem is not big desires, but small desires for big things."[31] Our desire for the biggest thing, the only thing that will truly satisfy us, is too small.

Our deepest longings and desires are not for romance, a wedding, marriage, or sex. If that's the case, where do they actually come from, and what do we most yearn for? If we look back to the Genesis account of our creation in the image of God, we remember that we were created out of the Love of the Trinity. The source of our lives is the union and communion flowing through the Trinitarian relationship. Since this is the case, clearly our longings originate from this place, and all other desires for romance and sex mask the deeper need. If we are to find life that truly satisfies, we must reinterpret these longings as invitations into love and communion with God.

What, then, is the meaning of marriage? The marital relationship provides a picture of deeper truths about God and ourselves. This relationship is not our ultimate destination in life, despite all that the culture around us espouses as true. Earthly marriage and sex can never satisfy us fully, and yet they are clearly part of the picture given to us by God to help us comprehend his invitation to perfect Love, communion, and even ecstasy.

How do we introduce these truths to the children in our lives? It is so important to establish foundational thinking that will be the basis of life-giving choices in the future. We can start by helping them identify and articulate their longings for love and connection, directing them to God as the One who can truly satisfy.

**SCRIPTURE**

*Surely your goodness and unfailing love will pursue me all the days of my life.* (Psalm 23:6, NLT)

**YOU CAN TELL YOUNGER CHILDREN**

1. God planned from the beginning to give us pictures that could help us to understand the ways he loves us.

2. One of the pictures God gave us is the picture of marriage.

3. This picture of marriage helps us to understand that God is inviting us into a relationship with him that can satisfy our deepest longings.

4. In what ways does God love you through the actions of your friends and family?

**YOU CAN TALK WITH OLDER KIDS**

1. Romance, sex, and marriage are only pictures of God's invitation into a beautiful and satisfying relationship with himself. They are just a part of the story.

2. When we seek any of these three "pictures" instead of God himself, we will be disappointed and perhaps even get hurt. Can you think of examples from stories, movies, or real life when someone got hurt because he or she was pursuing romance, sex, or marriage in order to be happy?

3. Read these words from C.S. Lewis together:

It would seem that Our Lord finds our desires not too strong but too weak. We are half-hearted creatures, fooling about with drink and sex and ambition when infinite joy is offered us, like an ignorant child who wants to go on making mud pies in a slum because he cannot imagine what is meant by the offer of a holiday at sea. We are far too easily pleased.[32]

Summarize by saying, "God is not asking us to ignore our desires, but to redirect them to the only one who can truly satisfy those desires."

**ACTIVITIES**

1. Find a travel poster or picture of a destination that the child longs to visit.

2. Ask the child if he or she would be happy with just putting that poster up on the wall in their bedroom instead of actually visiting the destination. What is the difference between these two options?

3. Read Ephesians 5:31-32 together. Talk with the child or kids about marriage as God's invitation to us to find the ultimate satisfaction of all that we long for in him. Draw your own travel poster that shows all that God is offering us in relationship with him. Write the words of Ephesians 5:31-32 at the top.

**PRAY TOGETHER**

*"God, I love you so much. Please help me to love you more. I want to live an epic love story with you. Amen."*

# Chapter 12

## What's Sex Got to Do with It?

### Linda Noble

Weddings can be simple, extravagant, excruciatingly long, delightful, or the best party of the year! My (Linda Noble) favorite wedding surprise was one that commenced with a procession of bridesmaids and groomsmen each playing an unusual instrument while strolling down the grassy center aisle beneath towering shade trees. In the olden days of the '70s we all had pretty much the same wedding: songs, slideshows, cake, sherbet ginger ale punch, nuts, and mints. I love that many weddings today are intentionally planned in a way that expresses something of who the bride and groom are as persons. I'm sure it's not hard to guess some of the particular personality traits of the couple hosting the aforementioned wedding.

In an effort to showcase the individuality and unique nature of the persons entering into marital union, couples last year spent an average of $33,390 per wedding.[33] Esther Lee, who wrote an article entitled "The Top Wedding Trends for 2021," names these among the top ten:

- "mini d'oeuvres"
- tiny toasts
- mismatched seating
- bistro-style entertainment
- coordinated guest dress codes
- living room decor[34]

Perhaps of most interest to me are the latest creative suggestions for ceremony elements that make a statement and symbolically reflect the joining of the couple in inseparable union. During my own wedding many years ago, we asked our parents to light the two outside candles displayed in a line of three placed in a candelabra. My husband-to-be and I, at just the right moment, together lit the center candle—without lighting my veil on fire—but made the grave mistake of failing to blow out our "family" candles, as is the custom. Maybe this is the source of all of our marital difficulties!

Unity ceremonies are not uncommon in weddings today. My reading up on this topic revealed the following as visible and physical expressions signifying the invisible union of two unique individuals:

- tree planting unity ceremony
- handmade basket exchange
- family puzzle unity ceremony
- painted canvas unity ceremony
- unity tea ceremony
- wine blending unity ceremony
- whiskey pouring unity ceremony, and...
- the UNITY VOLCANO

Will someone please invite me to a wedding with a unity volcano?

But seriously, as couples enter into the events of our wedding day, we all experience a deep desire to, in some way, express that we, as unrepeatable and irreplaceable persons, are entering with our whole selves into union with another. We intuitively are drawn to proclaim this invisible union through a visible sign. Why?

Let's talk about the biblical roots of the wedding ceremony. After all, the whole idea of a wedding ceremony originated with our designer and creator, God. To do this, we'll need to look at an important term, covenant: "The preferred meaning of this Old Testament word is bond; a covenant refers to two or more parties bound together."[35]

I encourage you to use this term, even though it may begin as unfamiliar, when you discuss these topics with the kids in your life. The practice of covenant-making was common in the Eastern cultures in Old Testament times. God calls upon this cultural practice to describe a way of entering into a relationship with his people in a way that is familiar to them.

An excerpt from *Bible Study Tools* explains the elements of a covenant this way:

Combining statements made in different accounts, the following seem to be the principal elements in a covenant between men…:

1. A statement of the terms agreed upon. (Genesis 26:29; 31:50, 52)

2. An oath by each party to observe the terms, God being witness of the oath (Genesis 26:31, 31:48-53). The oath was such a characteristic feature that sometimes the term "oath" is used as the equivalent of covenant. (See Ezekiel 17:13)

3. A curse invoked by each one upon himself in case of disregard of the agreement. In a sense this may be considered a part of the oath, adding emphasis to it. This curse is not explicitly stated in the case of human covenants, but may be inferred from the covenant with God. (Deuteronomy 27:15-26)

4. The formal ratification of the covenant by some solemn external act.[36]

Throughout Scripture, God describes his own relationship with his people as a covenantal marriage. When he speaks of marriage, he never makes reference to it as anything other than covenantal (see Jeremiah 31:31-33; Malachi 2:13-14; Isaiah 54:5; 2 Corinthians 11:2; Hosea 2:19; Isaiah 62:3-5). As *Bible Gateway's* commentary on biblical themes states,

Marriage is used to describe the relationship between God and Israel in the Old Testament and between Jesus Christ and the church in the New Testament. Contemplating marriage deepens understanding of God's love for his people; examining God's covenant love for his people similarly enriches an understanding of marriage.[37]

In a covenantal marriage, the bride and groom are present and prepared to enter into a covenant. Vows or oaths are made to one another that convey some version of this statement: "I give myself totally, freely, and only to you. I am entering into union with you until death do us part." These oaths are integral parts of a covenant ceremony, in which the presence of God is invoked, creating a permanent, mystical, and invisible bond between the bride and groom. Just as we see in the biblical examples, an external act is necessary in order to complete the covenant. Is there a unity ceremony that seals this union of two persons with a physical and visible sign and completes the covenant? Absolutely! The sexual union of the couple is the unity ceremony.

So here we have it: What is sex? It is designed to be the REAL DEAL unity ceremony. It is the physical sign sealing the vows or oaths of the covenantal marriage and signifying an inseparable union under the conditions of the covenant.

When questioned about divorce, Jesus first challenges the religious leaders who are looking for a new rule regarding marriage and refuses to accommodate them. He then points back to God's original design as described in the Genesis account and identifies the union of man and woman as a marriage (Matthew 19:4-6). Jesus teaches that the completion of this first marital covenant is not merely a sexual union, but is the union of two whole persons. This makes so much sense when we remember, from chapter 7, that we cannot separate the human body from the person. As a couple seals their covenantal vows with a visible sign (sex), they have become no longer two persons, but one.

What are the implications of this? As you might remember, we are moving beyond "the rules" and into a vision of God's design for a life of flourishing. The choices we make regarding sexual activity have more impact on us than we may recognize. It is our hope that we now leave all past mistakes and misunderstandings behind in order to live into a new vision of our lives with God. Our next chapter will explore and expand this idea further as we consider the language that our bodies speak.

CONVERSATIONS

**SCRIPTURE**

*"For the Lord your God is a compassionate God; He will not fail you nor destroy you nor forget the covenant with your fathers which He swore to them."* (Deuteronomy 4:31, NASB)

**YOU CAN TELL YOUNGER CHILDREN**

1. A covenant is a very serious promise or agreement. In the Bible, we read that God made covenants with his people. Each one of these covenants was sealed or completed by a visible sign. Maybe the most well-known covenant was the one that God made with Noah in the story of the ark. A rainbow is the visible sign that God will always keep this very serious promise.

2. The covenant that two people make during a wedding is a promise that they will be united for the rest of their lives.

3. They then will become close in a way that is very special for a husband and wife. Their bodies speak this message, "I give myself freely, totally, and only to you. I am becoming one with you until our lives are over."

**YOU CAN TALK WITH OLDER KIDS**

1.  At a wedding, two people come together before God and friends to enter into a life-long covenant in which they give their whole selves to one another. (Even though covenant is an unfamiliar word, it is useful to teach this terminology to children as it is fundamental to understanding Jesus's teaching on marriage.) Sex is the visible sign of this covenant for the married couple as it speaks of the complete union of husband and wife.

2.  During a wedding, we speak vows to one another. Later, the physical sign of this covenantal ceremony takes place as the couple experiences sexual union.

3.  What are some of the promises that you've heard spoken at weddings?

4.  This is one version of the traditional promise, or vow, given at a wedding: "I give myself freely, totally, and only to you. I am becoming one with you until our lives are over." If a couple were to take this promise seriously, how might it affect their marriage?

## ACTIVITIES

1. Do the volcano experiment with children as described here: http://www.lovemyscience.com/makingavolcano.html Talk about the way that combining two individual substances, baking soda and vinegar, creates something totally other than and beyond the original substances. Discuss the ways this experiment can help us to understand the impact of a covenant made at a wedding by two individuals.

2. Take kids to a wedding, or watch one on YouTube. Ask kids to identify the vows made at the wedding. If there is a unity ceremony, point this out and comment on the ways that it is a visible picture of the covenant vows that the two are making.

3. Research covenants made in the Bible. If you need help, look up Genesis 9:1-17 to discover more about God's covenant with Noah or Genesis 17 and the covenant of circumcision.

   • Identify the two parties involved.

   • Identify the solemn promise made.

   • Identify the visible sign that completed the promise.

## PRAY TOGETHER

*"God, thank you for your Love for us. Thank you for your Love for me. I want to give myself freely and fully to you. I was made to be in close relationship with you. Please help me to keep moving closer and closer to you. Amen."*

# Chapter 13

## The Language of the Body: Helping You to Talk About Sex
## Linda Stewart

Does an alarm go off in your head when your child or a kid whom you mentor is trying to pull one over on you? One of my closest childhood friends and I (Linda Stewart) were just kids when she told me that she could tell that I wasn't being truthful when my nostrils would flare. I was so bummed that my nose (of all things) gave me away! My own kids have "tells" that I won't make public, but I know them when I see them. I can actually picture it: the particular expression on each one's face when something's up, the way her posture changes. Seriously, take a minute and visualize the signs that give away that there might be more to what your kid, a child you know, or a friend is telling you. These kinds of visible giveaways can highlight genuineness, too: Visualize someone close to you so thrilled and excited or in awe that it is written all over his or her face. When my husband finds something really funny, his face breaks into total joy with his eyes crinkling, his shoulders rising up, and his mouth opening for a spontaneous laugh. I can absolutely picture him even as I type this. *The body communicates in its own language! Our body and our voice can agree or disagree.*

There are moments when my daughter speaks and her body sends a different message than her words do. In cases when I notice that something is out of sync, I tend to pay more attention to her body language. Similarly, when a client is speaking in my therapy room, I not only pay attention to the words, but also observe his or her body language. We all notice what people are communicating in these two different frequencies. We listen to the verbal communication, and we monitor the messages as they are expressed through the body. When there is a disparity between a person's verbal story and the body's visible communication, we might hesitate, wondering about the authenticity of the message. We often feel confused over mismatches, even in moments when the verbal message is positive or when that which is displayed through the body seems good. Why would this make us uncomfortable or wary? Because, as Linda Noble says in our in-person workshops, "This was God's intention from the beginning—that our bodies and our voices would speak in sync with his design." It seems that we inherently know this to be true, as evidenced by the way we (some of us more consciously and consistently than others) gauge whether the message of the body and the voice are in unison. This goes for all of us: single or married, children or adults. My body and my person are inseparable, and they contribute to the flourishing of others and myself when they speak in agreement as one.

The body has a language that's as expressive of our whole person as our voice is. We all—our kids included—flourish when the language of our body is in sync with the messages we speak with our voices. As parents or mentors to youth, the idea that our body speaks a language has numerous implications for kids of any age.

To build upon the last chapter, I'll suggest here that since the body speaks a language that is designed to be in sync with what's expressed through our words, parents and mentors can provide profound answers to the questions, "How far is too far?" and "Why does it matter if I have sex before marriage?" In the last chapter we explored the idea of the marriage covenant. *If* we embrace that idea, we recognize that marriage is so much more than signing a piece of paper. And similarly, sex is so much more than just a physical act that can occur in or outside of marriage.

Let's look more at what is happening in the marriage covenant. *(Before that, a note: If you are giving "the sex talk" or working with kids, please don't hesitate to use the word covenant. It's the only term we have that fully and accurately depicts the invisible reality behind the events taking place in a marriage ceremony.)*

In the entirety of the marriage covenant, the *voice* of each partner speaks the vows during the covenantal ceremony, and then the *body* of each partner physically speaks the same vows when the marriage is consummated. Sex is the physical and visible sign of the marriage covenant. Sex completes the covenantal vows by physically and visibly expressing what was spoken before God and others in the marriage ceremony: "I give myself totally, freely, and only to you. I am entering into union with you until death do us part."

How could this vision of sex as the visible sign of the marriage covenant change our conversations about sex and marriage? Christopher West illustrates the meaning of the language of the body by profoundly pointing out that every time a married couple has sex, they are restating or renewing their wedding vows.[38] The act of sexual union is full of significance.

All of this begs the question: What occurs in a sexual encounter that is *not* preceded by a covenantal promise of marriage? In that case, my voice and my body are in contradiction. To be more precise, my body speaks of lifelong union without my words providing the covenantal promise.

If this concept of discord is new for you, please know it was new to me too when I began to understand this as a part of *Theology of the Body*. If this brings up any challenging thoughts or uncomfortable feelings, please know there is absolutely no judgment here. That's not what this is about. We are simply inviting you at this moment to consider sex in light of the fact that the body has a language, and that as per our design, we flourish when our body and our voice speak in concert.

In other words, if the covenantal vows have been spoken along the lines of "I give myself totally, freely, and only to you; I am entering into union with you until death do us part," then the body affirms and seals these words when two embodied persons give themselves physically to each other totally, freely, and exclusively, entering into complete union until death do they part. This vision of total, free, exclusive, complete union is very profound, and as both a married woman and a therapist, I realize that it is easier said than done or experienced. However, it can be helpful to know what we were designed to aim for as this can allow us to take joy in the moments that we enjoy a taste of it, or to hold on to God tightly when disappointed that we haven't.

When the body speaks a covenantal message of lifelong union that contradicts words spoken (or omitted), this is damaging to the Self and to the other. Although most of the time we wouldn't think of it this way, *Theology of the Body* invites us to consider that sex without a covenantal promise is harmful because our words and what our body is saying are not in sync. The message and experience are, in fact, not total, free, exclusive, or complete. Feelings of insecurity, distrust, pain, and a fear of betrayal can occur in a sexual relationship outside of the marriage covenant. Yes, these feelings can be experienced within marriage as well, especially if or when what one or both partners' bodies speak (sexually or otherwise) is not in accord with the covenant made.

Remember, the objective of this book is to provide you with a vision to introduce to young people. Even this conversation about the meaning of sex is not about presenting rules about sex, but intended to offer an understanding of what sex is in light of the entire conversation of how to move in a direction of flourishing according to God's design. An excerpt from THE Conversation Workshop syllabus provides a talking point that is helpful here as you talk with kids about sex and bodies: "Because we are whole persons, our body-selves speak through our actions. When our bodies speak something different than our voices, there is confusion, hurt, and disappointment." When what we say with our bodies and our words aligns according to our design, it is possible to avoid some of this damage or hurt.

Incorporating the language of the body into our conversations about sex allows for a depth and breadth of conversation that is in stark contrast to "Don't have sex before marriage," or "Don't have sex unless you're ready."

It's important to remember that the concept of the language of the body is most helpful when it's been introduced long before any conversation about sex. These are topics we encourage you to discuss well in advance of when sex becomes a conversation point. On the other hand, if you've already had "the sex talk" we encourage you to introduce and use this idea of the language of the body to provide further clarity and depth to the meaning of sex.

CONVERSATIONS

## SCRIPTURE

*But the one who joins himself to the Lord is one spirit with Him.* (I Corinthians 6:17, NASB)

## YOU CAN TELL YOUNGER CHILDREN

1. Because we are whole persons, our body-selves speak through not just our words but also our actions.

2. My body can speak Jesus's Love to others.

3. We all recognize that our bodies speak. Often we hear someone speak with a voice, but his or her body contradicts the message spoken. Have you ever experienced something like this? How did you feel about it?

## YOU CAN TALK WITH OLDER KIDS

1. During a wedding, the voices of the bride and groom speak vows that describe their intention to join their whole selves in total union with one another until death parts them. The physical sign of this covenantal ceremony takes place as the couple experiences the act of sexual union. Sexual union is the language of the body that speaks of the covenant made.

2. Every time a married couple has sex, they are renewing their wedding vows.

3. So when we join our bodies to another outside of a covenant spoken in a marriage ceremony, there is a disconnect between our words and actions. Our bodies have spoken the language of total union for life, but we have not spoken the words of the marital covenant. What are some of the doubts and fears that result after an unmarried couple engages in sex? After talking about this, ask: Why do you think it's so painful when a couple breaks up after engaging in sex?

## ACTIVITIES

1. Read *Every Body Has Something to Say* by Monica Ashour with kids fourth grade and younger.

2. Talk about Jesus and the way he expressed Love to people with his body-self.

   How did he show Love with his hands? His legs? His mouth? His ears?

3. Talk about three ways each child can show God's Love with his or her body this week. Have the child fill in the blanks of this sentence: "I can use my _____ to show God's Love to _____ by _____." Draw a picture together illustrating each of the three sentences you wrote.

4. For older kids you might want to talk about movies or television shows that depict the pain that follows when words and actions are in contradiction.

## PRAY TOGETHER

*"God, thank you for creating my whole Self. Thank you for my body. Thank you that my body has its own way of speaking. Thank you that my body can speak your Love. Thank you that my arms can hug, my mouth can smile and say 'I love you,' my body can protect others, and my feet and legs can help me to bring things to my friends and family. I love you, Jesus! Amen."*

# Chapter 14

## Single Celibacy: Our Unexamined Presuppositions Are Hurting Us!

### Linda Noble

As a socially awkward and introverted teenager, I (Linda Noble) was ecstatic when I found belonging in a thriving high school youth group in the San Francisco Bay Area. I grew in confidence and leadership in this biblically-centered environment and received so many good gifts from God there. But as with everything in life, these good gifts came in a mixed bag. Once I established a circle of supportive and fun female relationships, I discovered that it was kind of "a thing" there to start a Hope Chest: a chest full of household items that would be joyfully unpacked WHEN one got married and established her own household. Among this group of young women, it was our idea of a good time to visit department stores, making decisions about our future dish patterns and household color schemes and planning purchases for our chests!

Each year, we anticipated the upcoming sex and dating teaching series in youth group. We eagerly sat on the edge of our seats as we listened to the speaker tell us that sex in marriage is awesome beyond imagination. Our interpretation of the message was this: "Get married so you can experience life's highest good with God's stamp of approval!" Many of us did get married young and quickly, as this seemed the best strategy for following "the rules" and at the same time satisfying what appeared to us to be our deepest longings and desires.

I don't remember ever hearing a talk on the beauty of the single and celibate life. In fact, I'm not sure, forty-five years later, that I have ever heard a talk in a Protestant context extolling the incredible possibilities of this type of life. As I think about it, I find it strange that we hungrily study Jesus's life in detail but ignore the fact that he lived a life of abundance, joy, and meaning as a single, celibate male. Is that really humanly possible?

In a 2011 *Christianity Today* article titled "Solitary Refinement," Lauren Winner comments, "There is very little space in today's evangelical churches for discerning a call to singleness. Catholics—at least Catholics who believe they are called not just to celibacy but also to religious orders—have something positive to do..."[39] Winner has a great point. In the Catholic context we can identify a high value imparted to the person who chooses to forgo life with a human partner for a partnership with God and his work in our world. Instead of casting a vision in our church communities for a meaningful and satisfying life for our single friends who choose celibacy, the evangelical church has a tendency to shove them into the corner room in a singles ministry and hope they find their soulmates so they can be happy like us married people.

How did the Protestant church arrive at this position? Jeremy Erickson sheds light on the origins of our attitudes in his article "Protestant Opposition to Celibacy," where he states, "Historically speaking, Protestant criticism of celibacy dates as far back as the Reformation itself. Several of the early Protestant Reformers such as Luther criticized the Catholic mandate that priests be celibate."[40]

In an article entitled "The Reformation and the Reform of Marriage," Susan Mobley from Concordia University reaches this conclusion: "During the Reformation, then, Catholics and Protestants came to have different views on marriage. Protestants abolished the religious ideal of celibacy and replaced it with an elevated view of marriage."[41] Somewhere along the way, as the first Protestants protested Catholic teaching, the value of the single celibate life got lost in an overemphasis on marriage and family that we experience in many of our churches today.

Many churches plan a yearly sermon series that highlights marriage and family without regard to the message this sends to single members. As I've listened to pastoral messages in other seasons, I have come to a new sensitivity to the vast number of illustrations that involve stories of the speaker's life as a husband, wife, or parent. Although these are not intended to disregard the value of the single person's vocation, silence on the topic of the beauty of this vocation speaks volumes.

It seems to me that unwittingly we've allowed ourselves as Christ-followers to be sucked into the same conviction that our culture now assumes to be truth: that sex is an essential element to human flourishing, a key part of a satisfying and fulfilling life. And because we as Christ-followers believe the Bible teaches that marriage is the proper context for sex, the popular Christian perspective interprets marriage to be—at some level of our consciousness—a prerequisite for a satisfying and fulfilling life. As a result, the focus in our church communities tends to center on fortifying marriages. Often the very reason that marriages are failing is that they cannot support this expectation. Perhaps, as Christ-followers, both single and married, there is something MORE essential to a life that flourishes than sex or marriage, and we've failed to call it out.

If that's not problematic enough, strangely we as Christians have also fallen in step with the belief that sex and sexual pleasure are animal impulses that cannot realistically be denied. We hear this implied by marriage speakers who exhort wives to satisfy their husbands' sexual needs so that they will not stray. Youth educators often place the responsibility for the lusts of young men on our girls as a motivation for dressing modestly.

In my conversations with young singles at church, the prevailing attitude is this: "God gave me sexual desires and it's certainly not possible that he has an unrealistic expectation that I should deny those." If this is what we believe, then to encourage any single person to live the celibate life that's consistent with biblical teaching is to inflict cruel and unusual punishment upon them. Jeremy Erickson observes additional fallout from this assumption:

Lack of marriage can be viewed with suspicion, as an indication that people are likely to fall to sexual sin. Some even argue that failure to marry is a sinful shirking of adult responsibility. Underlying much of this attitude is the belief that for the vast majority of people, celibacy is either impossible or cannot be fulfilling...Many Protestants see celibate living as a needless source of loneliness, and as the sort of thing that can be viewed as a form of punishment. On the other hand, they see marriage as the universal solution to the problems of loneliness and sexual temptation.[42]

I think, if we're honest, we recognize these statements as reflections of our unexamined, unspoken, and perhaps unrecognized beliefs.

This failure to realize the error in adopting the attitudes of our culture and Christianizing them is taking us down a road that leads to confusion and destructive choices that our kids will also face. The reality of the situation is explained by Katelyn Beaty in *Same-Sex Marriage and the Single Christian*:

Marriage—and with it, sexual fulfillment and companionship and the possibility of children—is not a guarantee in this life, far less a fundamental right. Rather, it is a gift and a vocation, given to many but not all, it seems. And with all the dust in the air about prolonged adolescence and man-boys and women outpacing men in schools and the workforce, marriage is no longer the shoo-in it was for most Christian women of my parents' and grandparents' generation. That includes me.[43]

Our kids will face singleness at one point or another in their lives. How will they navigate their single seasons if we don't rethink what we teach and imply about singleness?

Our thoughtless approach urgently needs to be addressed! Our response to the challenge of reenvisioning a life of flourishing apart from sex and marriage has huge implications for our kids. We MUST answer questions like these:

*Is marriage the solution for loneliness and companionship?*

*Is marriage the antidote to lust?*

*Can one live a single celibate life without being miserable?*

*Is there beauty in a single and celibate life? If so, what does it look like?*

*Can one encourage a friend to follow Jesus in a single celibate lifestyle and still be considered a loving and compassionate person?*

*Is there a way to enjoy loving friendship without entering into a sexual relationship?*

*Do we need to make radical changes in our church communities in order to be family to our single and celibate friends?*

We believe that we can find answers within the teachings of Pope John Paul II's *Theology of the Body.*

## CONVERSATIONS

### SCRIPTURE

*But I want you to be free from concern. One who is unmarried is concerned about the things of the Lord, how he may please the Lord; but one who is married is concerned about the things of the world, how he may please his wife, and his interests are divided. The woman who is unmarried, and the virgin, is concerned about the things of the Lord, that she may be holy both in body and spirit; but one who is married is concerned about the things of the world, how she may please her husband. This I say for your own benefit; not to put a restraint upon you, but to promote what is appropriate and to secure undistracted devotion to the Lord.* (1 Corinthians 7:32-35, NASB)

*For it is written,*
*"Rejoice, barren woman who does not bear;*
*Break forth and shout, you who are not in labor;*
*For more numerous are the children of the desolate*
*Than of the one who has a husband."* (Galatians 4:27, NASB)

### YOU CAN TELL YOUNGER CHILDREN

1. Use the phrases, "If you get married" and "If you have children" rather than assuming that they will ("When you get married" and "When you have children").

2. Refrain from entering into the role of matchmaker with your single friends. Talk about them in a manner that highlights the ways they are using their gifts and abilities to show love to people in the world around them. If you are married, remind yourself and the kids you are talking with that your status as married is not a superior one, just different.

3. Talk to children about practical ways to show Jesus's kind of Love to those in the world around them. Make sure that the conversations are inclusive of classmates and neighbors of both genders.

**YOU CAN TALK WITH OLDER KIDS**

1.  We often fall prey to feeling sorry for those who are not married, and yet Jesus experienced the abundant kind of life apart from sex and marriage. A life of flourishing is experienced by people living both the vocation of singleness and the vocation of marriage. How can we think about all of this differently by looking at the life of Jesus?

2.  We respect and celebrate vocations of marriage and single celibacy as the calling and invitation of God, with eagerness to learn from one another. Who are some married people you admire? Who are some single people you admire? What qualities do they have in common?

3.  Avoid a hyper focus on relationships and dating with your kids and with others. Don't ask, "Why aren't you married? or "Any cute guys or girls in your class?"

**ACTIVITIES**

1.  Highlight the lives of single persons you know and the works of love they are doing in the world.

2.  Draw the outline of a human form on a large paper. Entitle it "Jesus Loves." Remind children that Jesus lived his life on earth as a human person who never married. Read one of the Gospels out loud over a period of a week and ask the child(ren) you're talking with to identify ways that Jesus loved people. Write those descriptions on the human outline you've drawn.

3.  Invite singles into your family and home, affirming them as persons and welcoming the gifts they bring.

**PRAY TOGETHER**

*"God, thank you so much for every good thing you have made. Please show me the adventures that you are inviting me to participate in with you. Please help me to know your voice and recognize your invitations to goodness and flourishing during every season of my life. Amen."*

If you want to include the message of this chapter more explicitly, you can add to the prayer: *"Please show me which adventures you're calling me to when I'm single, and help me to know if and when you call me to be married. Amen."*

# Chapter 15

## Practical Help for Elevating Our Views on the Single and Celibate Life

### Linda Noble

As we've seen in our previous chapters and in our workshop, THE Conversation raises some serious questions regarding popular Christian teaching surrounding marriage, sex, sexual purity, and single celibacy.

The unspoken and underlying assumptions the Christian church has embraced:

- Marriage, and sex in the context of marriage, are prerequisites for a satisfying and fulfilling life.
- Single celibacy is a sentence for a life of deprivation and loneliness.

These assumptions not only contradict biblical teaching but are the source of pain, resentment, and many destructive choices:

- Our single and celibate friends feel God has cheated them and desperately seek to get married.
- Many who are single would argue that a good God who wants good things for us could not possibly expect celibacy, as this is an absurdly cruel and unusual punishment.
- Those in church leadership who promote a celibate life for those who are single, as unmarried, divorced, widowed, or same-sex-attracted Christ-followers, are viewed as dogmatic, irrelevant, and uncompassionate because of all of the negatives we associate with a single life.

- Our children absorb and observe these attitudes, and by the time they are faced with their own choices regarding sexuality and marriage, many fall into the traps we've unwittingly created as a result of our failure to align our assumptions with biblical teaching on single celibacy. As a mother of adult children, I've seen this firsthand as friends encounter these same protests from their children who grew up in church environments.

I (Linda Noble) would like to suggest some ideas for course correction. After all, how is it helpful to point out the problem without offering practical solutions? You'll probably recall that we've been laying a foundation for a descriptive approach to God's design for the body, sex, and relationships. We start by nurturing this perspective in the children we influence. Beyond this, we can also make intentional changes to the way we talk about marriage and singleness. The following are some suggestions that can help us elevate the vocation of single celibacy in our home and church environments:

- As was suggested in the previous chapter, use phrases like, "If you get married…" and "If you have children…" rather than assuming that this will be the future of our children and youth or single friends. This change communicates that the vocation of marriage is not an expectation for their lives.

- Authentically share the ways God is satisfying your biggest needs as a person. Talk about his very personal words spoken to you, his gifts that you receive, the moments of love and comfort that you experience with him. Try to avoid using churchy language in your descriptions in order to create interest and avoid immediate dismissal of your words. Keep your words as conversational and genuine as possible.

- Watch movies and television together, listen to music together, and read together. When you observe a character seeking human love as the ultimate experience in life, point out with compassion that human love can never truly satisfy our deep need for the perfect Love for which we are made.

- Point out to young people that Jesus calls us to love others. We are invited to love others with Jesus's self-giving Love apart from a sexual or marital relationship. A single and celibate life does not have to be a life devoid of Love.

- Avoid a hyper focus on relationships and dating with your kids and with others. Don't ask "Why aren't you married?" or "I wonder why he/she isn't married?" Don't ask your kids, "Are there any cute boys/girls in your class?" And certainly, stop trying to find partners for single friends.

- Do not label or isolate people by relationship status. Instead, model discovering each person you encounter as a whole person, refusing to define him or her as single or married. Focus on uncovering the unique ways each one reflects the image of God.

- Invite singles into your family and/or home, affirming them as persons and welcoming the gifts they bring. Our family has three "adopted" family members who are single. We aren't doing them a favor, by the way. God has used each of them to bring beautiful and irreplaceable gifts to our lives. At the same time, they get to experience all the ongoing joys and trials of being part of a family and investing in the lives of the children who call them aunt or uncle.

- Encourage your kids to develop intimacy with God. Ask them these questions regularly: "Where did God show up for you this week?" "What good gifts did God bring you today?" "When have you felt closest to God lately?"

- Read stories with children about the lives of those heroes of the faith who found abundant and satisfying life with God as single and celibate persons.

Maybe most importantly, we need to ask ourselves this question: Are we convinced that it is really possible to live a full and satisfying life as a single celibate person? We might be surprised by our own answers.

If we are going to teach our youth to truly trust and have confidence in God's direction for the celibate life of a single person, it is absolutely necessary to communicate to them that life as a celibate person can be beautiful and satisfying, possibly even more beautiful and satisfying than the life of a married person. We can't stop there, but continue to mentor them and help them to move toward an experience of God that gives them hope that this is actually true.

I'll close with these words used to describe the God-filled life of Brother Lawrence, a monk who labored in a monastery kitchen and repaired sandals for forty-nine years:

> He is now so accustomed to that Divine presence that he receives from it continual comfort and peace. For about thirty years his soul has been filled with joy and delight so continual, and sometimes so great, that he is forced to find ways to hide their appearing outwardly to others who may not understand."[44]

Yes, Brother Lawrence! Teach us your ways!

CONVERSATIONS

## SCRIPTURE

*Because your love is better than life, my lips will glorify you. I will praise you as long as I live, and in your name I will lift up my hands. I will be fully satisfied as with the richest of foods; with singing lips my mouth will praise you.* (Psalm 63:3-5, NIV)
(For little ones: "My lips will glorify you" means "I will tell God and others how wonderful he is and how wonderful his Love is.")

## YOU CAN SAY TO YOUNGER CHILDREN

1. Authentically share how you and God are connecting in ways that deeply satisfy you. Talk about God speaking his Love to you through Scripture, worship experiences, art, or nature where God met you in a particularly beautiful way.

2. Ask the child to talk about the moments when he or she feels most loved by God.

3. Talk about the disappointment we experience when humans don't love us the way we wish they would. What do you think God wants to say to us in those moments?

**YOU CAN TALK WITH OLDER KIDS**

1. Encourage him or her to develop intimacy with God. Regularly ask questions like, "Where did God show up for you this week?" and "What good gifts have you received from God this week?"

2. Research and read about the lives of single and celibate Christians who have found beauty and meaning in their vocations. Some possible ideas are Brother Lawrence, Corrie ten Boom, Mother Teresa, Wesley Hill, Pope John Paul II, and Susan B. Anthony. Talk about the ways they experienced meaning and satisfaction as single persons.

3. Discuss the expectations people have for romantic relationships.

   • What happens when one of the partners cannot meet those expectations?

   • How might a close relationship with Jesus help when the expectations we have of people are not met?

**ACTIVITIES**

1. Do a study of Jesus's life, looking for Scripture that describes the ways he met the emotional and material needs of those who were around him.

2. Watch videos of worship songs, or listen to worship music together. Talk about words from the songs that express God's Love to us. Ask which words or phrases the child finds most meaningful.

3. Using all that you've discovered from the previous activities in this book, create a Valentine from God to the child. Work on this Valentine together, perhaps writing on it Scripture or a phrase from a song, or write your own letter describing God's Love for him or her.

**PRAY TOGETHER**

*"God, thank you that you ARE Love and the Source of the Love that I crave. When my life is nice, and when my life is hard, please remind me always that you like to fill me up with so much of your Love that it spills over. Please fill me up with your Love today. Amen."*

## Chapter 16

### Rethinking Lust
### Linda Noble

About five years ago, I (Linda Noble) found myself in the audience at a marriage retreat organized by our church. To be completely honest, I have never enjoyed marriage retreats; they seem to ignite in me an overwhelming sense of failure and hopelessness. However, that's beside the point I want to make here! That day, all of us participating entered the meeting room where the presenters sat side by side up on the platform, the wife smiling and looking adoringly at her husband. The topic was the beauty of marital sex. When the woman stood to address the crowd, she began to admonish wives to satisfy their husband's lusts as a safeguard against their use of pornography and extramarital affairs. After all, we can't possibly expect men to avoid sin unless their wives satisfy these needs. My eyebrows raised, my internal alarms began sounding, and anger welled up inside of me. Following the session, a twenty-something couple approached me. The young man insightfully remarked, "I think I've just been called an animal by the retreat speaker! I'm offended!" In that moment, I was given words to verbalize my revulsion to this very common message to wives in Christian contexts.

Let's go back into the book of Genesis. Reading the story of the beginnings of the human person has been helpful in our discovery of God's design thus far. Jesus himself pointed his questioners back to this same account in seeking to correct faulty views of marriage (Matthew 19:3-4). In Genesis 1 and 2, we see the first two human persons, beautiful reflections of God's image, walking and talking together with him in an idyllic setting. In the teaching of *Theology of the Body*, we learned that there was no threat to the dignity and value of the other as a human person. Each viewed the other as a beautiful and unique creation of God and related to him as such. Christopher West explains this further: "This is what Adam and Eve experienced 'in the beginning.' The very sentiment of sexual desire as God created it to be was to love as God loves in the sincere gift of self."[45] They image God together, experiencing a life of giving and receiving and returning love to one another. They are naked and not ashamed.

In Genesis 3, a disruption of this loving relationship occurs when the serpent approaches them, offering an alternative to this way of living. This serpent implies that God certainly was withholding the best life from them. It proposes that they grasp for themselves that which could REALLY satisfy their desires. The ultimate result of this grasping is disordered relationships as they begin to turn to view one another as objects to satisfy their own desires. The first couple now knows that their self-inflicted brokenness opened the door for them to become victims or perpetrators of use and abuse. Lust made its entrance into our world and they cover their nakedness for protection from one another. Blame, shame, and suspicion have entered into the picture, and they hide from God and each other.

I did some reading on the current Christian cultural understanding of the word "lust." The definitions are all over the map, so for our purposes, I am going to draw a relationship between Pope John Paul's personalistic norm and lust. The personalistic norm states, "The person is a good towards which the only proper and adequate attitude is love."[46] Lust and God's kind of self-giving, self-sacrificing Love cannot coexist. There are no exceptions. We do not lay aside our call to image God's Love in order to experience intimate marital relations. The second piece of the personalistic norm describes lust: "The person cannot be treated as an object of use and as such the means to an end."[47] Using another human person (or even using our own body-selves) to satisfy our appetites is called lust, and it is a deep offense to love.

I find that men, and some women, have a hard time with this message. It is extremely difficult to imagine a life without lust, even in the context of marriage and relations with one's spouse. I sincerely believe that this is a result of our acceptance of lust as a natural part of the male life experience. Some would go so far as to say that God created men to be lustful. Our generally accepted solution for this inevitability is for men to marry and wives to do whatever it takes to satisfy their lusts. I would propose, though, that many women and men are offended by this "solution" at some level and much damage has ensued because of its failings.

This is not the only problem we've created for ourselves as we've unthinkingly accepted this assumption that lust cannot be avoided: If this is true, then the only solution for a Christ-follower to satisfy their lusts is marriage. Where does this leave our single and same-sex attracted friends whom we encourage to remain celibate?

What do I propose? C.S. Lewis states in *Mere Christianity* that "Love is the great conqueror of lust."[48] Christopher West explains the Pope's teaching in *Theology of the Body Explained*:

> To gain a true victory over lust, John Paul says that purity must mature from the negative turning away, to the more positive recognition and assertion of the real beauty, dignity and value of the body and sex. This can only happen through the concerted effort, in this case of the man, guided by grace, to see the woman's personhood revealed through her feminine body. Through the indwelling of the Holy Spirit, such "seeing" becomes not only a concept accepted by the mind but a living reality "felt" by the heart… [this happens] not perfectly in this life, but more and more effectively as we allow all of our diseased ways of thinking about the body and sexuality to be crucified with Christ.[49]

We must learn to see each other, even those we catch a glimpse of on the street, with God's eyes, and love each other with his Love! This is truly a transformational way to overcome lust!

What if we taught our children that they are not animals? What if we could be enabled to teach them to see and love the person revealed through the human body? What if we actually taught and trained our children from a young age that every human person is someone of value and worth, and that the only adequate attitude toward each one is love? What if we insisted that lust is never an appropriate attitude toward a human person? And what if we taught them the way to REALLY love?

## CONVERSATIONS

**SCRIPTURE**

*Love never gives up.*
*Love cares more for others than for self.*
*Love doesn't want what it doesn't have.*
*Love doesn't strut,*
*Doesn't have a swelled head,*
*Doesn't force itself on others,*
*Isn't always "me first,"*
*...Trusts God always,*
*Always looks for the best,*
*Never looks back,*
*But keeps going to the end.*
(1 Corinthians 13:4-7, MSG)

**YOU CAN SAY TO YOUNGER CHILDREN**

1. God is Love and he invites us to love like he does.

2. We all have things that we really want or think will make us happy, but these can keep us from loving well unless we learn how to depend on God for a joyful and flourishing life.

3. We choose to have an attitude of love toward family, friends, and others, knowing that love is what they are made for.

4. Using others to get what we want is not love.

**YOU CAN TALK WITH OLDER KIDS**

1. "The person is a good towards which the only proper and adequate attitude is love. The person cannot be treated as an object of use for the selfish pleasure of another."[50] Can you give some examples of moments when you've seen people being used or treated as an object?

2. We must begin to view others through a different lens. Each encounter with another human is an encounter with a person expressed through a body. Each body, whether ours and our neighbor's or a stranger's, is a temple of the Holy Spirit, a manifestation of divine beauty. In what ways would seeing others through this type of lens change dating relationships?

3. This perspective doesn't change whether we are married or single. Lust, use, and abuse are brokenness, both inside and outside the context of marriage.

4. When talking about dating relationships, ask children to consider questions like these: "What is it that I really want to get from this person?" "How might our relationships look different if I choose to love this person with Jesus's kind of Love rather than trying to get what I want from him or her?"

**ACTIVITIES**

1. Make a list of things that you really long for. Talk about how it feels in those moments when we don't get what we really long for. How do we feel when we don't get what we want from another person? Point out that using another person to get what we want is not love.

2. Write a thank you card or create a gift for someone who has loved you with Jesus's kind of Love.

3. Invite your child or the young people you mentor to fill in the blanks and then pray the following: "Hello, God. There are things that I want or things that it seems will make me happy. Thank you so much for _____, and giving me something I really wanted. And thank you so much that I can know you love me, even though I don't have _____. Sometimes I feel _____ when I can't have what I want. I want to want you more than anything or anyone in the world. Will you please fill me with your Love so that I can feel it even when I'm feeling _____ and _____ because I really want something I can't have."

**PRAY TOGETHER**

*"God, thank you that Jesus showed us how to love like you love. I'm asking you to please help me every day to have an attitude of love toward every person. Please remind me when I forget this and forgive me when I choose not to have an attitude of love. Thank you that every day I get to practice loving others the way that you do. Amen."*

If you want to include the message of this chapter more explicitly for older kids, you can add to the prayer: *"God, please give me your eyes to see those I'm attracted to. Please let the love that I experience when I see them as you do conquer any lust that wants to use them for myself. Amen."*

# Chapter 17

## What Fuel Are Our Kids Running On?

### Linda Stewart

So many of the choices kids make surrounding sex and relationships are motivated by the very real longings they experience. Sex and relationships can be false fuels that appear to help us achieve our deeper longings. If our kids learn to notice their most real longings and instead bring those longings to Jesus with the expectation that they'll be satisfied by the One who Truly Satisfies, they will be free to make different choices regarding sex and relationships. These are the choices that will lead to lives that flourish. As C.S. Lewis writes, "God designed the human machine to run on Himself. He Himself is the fuel our spirits were designed to burn, or the food our spirits were designed to feed on. There is no other."[51]

Let's briefly unpack this idea of false fuels and real longings, and consider some practical approaches to sharing God's Love with the kids in our lives.

Confession: I (Linda Stewart) know I was made to run on God's Love, but much of the time I believe that I can or should run on something else. I frequently try to fuel my body-self with what I urgently long for in the moment: TV, candy, food, coffee—and "relaxing" with said TV, candy, food, or coffee. None of these things is bad in and of itself, and sometimes these things really are gifts from God! Yet, even good gifts can unintentionally be grasped as the fuel that I *must have to be happy*. We can turn good things into false fuels if we forget that we were designed to run on God himself. False fuel is not what I truly long for, and it can never actually satisfy. At any given moment, a false fuel is just what I mistakenly believe (so strongly sometimes!) will satisfy the true ache of longing.

In the examples I've disclosed, the real ache that only God can satisfy might be that I am longing to feel taken care of or to be comforted. Life can at times *appear* to dictate that if I am longing to be comforted, then I need to provide the comfort for myself. So even something as good as food, rest, or great entertainment can be the thing that I grasp for or demand when I incorrectly think this experience itself is what sustains me. I'm choosing not to run on (or have forgotten) the fuel that is God himself. False fuel often sounds like this: "If I can just get enough rest, I'll be able to flourish." A false fuel can be anything (a behavior, belonging, experience, or person) good, harmful, or even neutral that we believe will fuel us in living our best life. Yet, anything other than God and his Love is unsustainable as fuel. It won't work in the long run, and can actually be destructive.

Our family is about to embark on our first trip to Utah. Road trip! We can, and will, bring along all kinds of items and goodies to enhance the experience. However, we will never get to Utah—and could need repairs on our car—if we attempt to get to our destination on anything other than gasoline. Likewise, there are countless good things that contribute to or even result from a flourishing life, but these are not the things on which we were designed to run. We really, truly can only run on God's Love. *In the same way, the kids we love can only run on God's Love.*

On what false fuels do the kids in your life attempt to run? Maybe you've heard something similar to the following:

- "If I had (fill in the blank with the toy or tech of the moment), I'd be happy forever."
- "If I could be in that friend group, everything would be better."

Or:

- "I can't really be happy unless I have a boyfriend/girlfriend."
- "I have to get accepted to this college for my life to work out."

- "Of course I'm having sex; my life wouldn't be normal and healthy if I wasn't."

These statements, and others like them, make golden moments because they provide opportunities for meaningful conversations. We can help our kids to recognize what they are really asking for and then coach them to direct their aches and longings to God for the kind of satisfaction only his Love provides.

We can help our kids learn to:

1. Recognize the longing.

   *Example: "When you picture life as being perfect with a boyfriend, what are you imagining it would look like? What longings do you have that it seems like a boyfriend could fulfill?"*

2. Choose not to grasp at people or things to satisfy a longing.

   *Example: "Wow, that sounds like something you want so badly. I'm so glad that we've already talked about never using someone else to get what we want. You always have a choice in how you treat others and I'm so glad that you work hard to not use other people, even to get a boyfriend."*

3. Direct longings to God for satisfaction.

   *Example: "Have you tried describing to God how you feel? He loves you so much. You can be honest and then ask him in what ways he wants to come through for you in this area that you are longing for. He really can satisfy and comfort you in this."*

Start today and develop a family culture that lovingly and supportively calls out attempts to put anything other than God's Love in our gas tank. Share age-appropriate examples with your kids of how God's Love satisfies you even in really difficult times.

### SCRIPTURE

*I've learned by now to be quite content whatever my circumstances. I'm just as happy with little as with much, with much as with little. I've found the recipe for being happy whether full or hungry, hands full or hands empty. Whatever I have, wherever I am, I can make it through anything in the One who makes me who I am.* (Philippians 4:11-13, MSG)

**YOU CAN SAY TO YOUNGER CHILDREN**

1. We all have things we really want or think will make us happy, but these can keep us from loving well unless we learn how to depend on God to satisfy us.

2. We can talk to God ANY time about the things we really want or feel like we have to have. He likes to hear about what we long for.

3. God's Love satisfies us and comforts us even in really difficult times.

**YOU CAN TALK WITH OLDER KIDS**

1. What are some of the things that you want, and why do you want them?

2. God's Love satisfies in an "already, but not yet" way—meaning that in this space after Eden and before Heaven we really can experience God's Love and the satisfaction of our longings, like Jesus did. And at the same time, because we are not yet in Heaven, we continue to reach for his Love and satisfaction in the moments or seasons when it feels harder to access him.

3. Can you remember a time when you got something you really wanted? How long did your happiness with that thing last?

4. Have you ever pulled an all-nighter? Or tried to go too long without sleep or without eating? Do you remember how that felt?

5. Sometimes we try to keep going without God. Have you noticed how it's affected you to go too long without being close to God?

**ACTIVITIES**

1.  You and your child or kids you mentor can both make a list of some of the longings you recognize in yourselves. Ask questions and be curious when kids talk about the longings they wrote down. You can let them know that God often gives us longings that help to bring us closer to him.

2.  Use *The Satisfaction of All My Desires* tool from the appendix of this book as a reminder that God's Love really does satisfy our deepest longings. Have kids highlight the desires that they have a difficult time believing God can fully satisfy. Invite kids to pray about the ones they highlighted by asking God to show them that he will in fact do what he says.

**PRAYER**

*"God, thank you that you designed me so that the only way I can really keep going in life is with you filling me. Please show me the times when I am trying to fill myself up with anything that is not you. Make my heart crave you more than I crave anything else. Amen."*

134

# Chapter 18

## What DOES Love Look Like?

### Linda Stewart

How many times has love been the rationale to sleep with someone, cohabitate, or end a marriage? How often has a woman or man been used or coerced with the words, "I love you," or "If you love me..."? The word "love" is used so frequently and so freely.

As parents, we use the word "love" to communicate the depth of feeling and commitment to our children. Adults also use the word "love" to offer kids a roadmap for decision-making. Thoughtful parents, caregivers, and mentors frequently use the word "love" with children while having "the sex talk," or in any of the myriad of conversations regarding relationships and dating. The following are examples shared with me (Linda Stewart) by two different parents:

"Sex is designed for a committed marital relationship in which two people really love each other."

"Wait to have sex until you find someone who you love."

Love is at the crux of what is being communicated to our kids about sex and relationships. As adults, we have something in mind when we use the word "love," but what do our children hear? Love is constantly being defined for youth by media, adults, and their peers. Many children have an incredibly murky view of what love is. Just because someone uses the word "love" doesn't mean that authentic love is being expressed.

We must intentionally define love for our kids (even our adult children), and we must be just as intentional in defining what love is not. As mentors and caregivers, we can offer young people an understanding that is defined by God's kind of Love. God's Love is the baseline kids can use to determine what really is love, and what is not.

**God is Love, and so we learn what love looks like from him:**

> This is how God showed His love for us: God sent his only Son into the world so we might live through Him. This is the kind of love we are talking about—not that we once upon a time loved God, but that he loved us and sent his Son as a sacrifice to clear away our sins and the damage they've done to our relationship with God.
> —1 John 4:7-10 (MSG)

**God provided us with a walking, talking picture of what love looks like through Jesus. Jesus's kind of Love:**

1. respects and affirms the image of God in all others.

2. is given freely, not forced and not demanded.

3. cares about the other's feelings.

4. does not use others to get what it wants.

As the Source and Sustainer of Real Love, Jesus's Love is what we must consistently expose our kids to. And remember, Jesus's kind of Love results in flourishing regardless of a person's status of single or married.

There are many ways this could be communicated to a child or young adult. One example is saying something like, "Our body-selves image God in a unique and unrepeatable way. Because this is true, we are to be treated with respect and with an attitude of love, and we choose to treat others with Jesus's kind of Love. This kind of Love respects and affirms the image of God in all others. This Love is given freely, not demanded or forced. Jesus's kind of Love cares about others' feelings. It doesn't use others to get what we feel that we need or want. Using is not love."

Knowing what love looks like makes it possible for our children to:

- choose to love others well.
- recognize when they are being treated lovingly.
- recognize when they are NOT being treated with love.

What a valuable gift! My daughters and I have mostly navigated questions of love from a perspective of friendship as well as through relationships at school and church. We might talk about things like:

- Is she treating others with love?
- Is she being treated with Jesus's kind of Love?
- When a friend or peer is not treating her with an attitude of love, is my daughter still choosing to love that person, knowing that love is what they (and she) are made for?

Not only does this understanding help to inform many types of relationships, it also communicates that use and abuse are not okay. The desired outcome is that if a child experiences another person as coercive (forcing him or her to do something), using him or her as an object, or not caring about his or her comfort or safety, that is not love. We want our kids to recognize for themselves that use and abuse are never appropriate or acceptable attitudes toward a person.

This conversation about love can begin in the earliest years. See Appendix B, "Teaching Kids What Love Doesn't Look Like," for a suggested script you can use or put into your own words in order to have a conversation with kids about how to recognize use and abuse. As the children in our lives practice recognizing real love in themselves and in others, this thought process will become a way of life, making it possible to revolutionize and transform their relationships.

CONVERSATIONS

### SCRIPTURE

*This is how God showed his love for us: God sent his only Son into the world so we might live through Him. This is the kind of love we are talking about—not that we once upon a time loved God, but that He loved us and sent his Son as a sacrifice to clear away our sins and the damage they've done to our relationship with God.* (1 John 4:7-10, MSG)

### YOU CAN TALK TO YOUNGER CHILDREN

1. The only proper attitude toward you is love.

2. The only proper attitude for you to have toward others is love.

3. Jesus shows us what real Love looks like.

4. You can recognize if you are being loved or if you are being loving by taking a look at Jesus's kind of Love.

5. As you think of Bible stories about Jesus, what do you remember about the ways he loved people?

**FOR OLDER CHILDREN**

*Talk to an older child about any concerns regarding a relationship in his or her life if you observe that the child is being treated coercively, without care, or if you see them being used. Consider this approach too if a teen or adult you care about seems negatively changed by or burdened by a relationship, or if you observe that they are not treating a relationship with Jesus's kind of Love.*

1. Invite the Holy Spirit to guide these conversations and listen for the Holy Spirit's guidance.

2. Communicate to the child: "You are not alone. We're in this together."

3. Make sure you've confirmed to this child that you see him or her as a person made in the image of God. Make sure they understand that love is the motivation for your conversation with them.

4. Ask your child or the person you mentor what he or she is longing for.

5. Talk about ways to release the other person from satisfying their longings and choosing to love like Jesus does.

6. Pray together, inviting God to meet their deepest longings.

**ACTIVITIES**

1. With your child or the kid(s) you mentor, create a poster with pictures or a list on paper of people in their world arranged across the top. Underneath each picture or name, create three rows.

2. In the first row, under the picture of each person, write reasons that it is sometimes hard to love this person.

3. In the second row, ask what he or she needs to sacrifice in order to love this person like Jesus does. Write it down.

4. In the third row, ask him or her to write one way he or she can love this person as Jesus does.

5. Review the poster with them after a week, asking about ways that he or she was able to love each one.

**PRAY TOGETHER**

*"God, thank you for showing us what real Love is. Please teach me to love with Jesus's kind of Love. And please help me to recognize when others are loving me with Jesus's kind of Love. Since you are the only One who can love me perfectly, I pray that I learn the most about Love from you. Amen."*

# Chapter 19

## THE Sex Talk

Thank you for journeying with us through the beautiful truths from *Theology of the Body* that have informed the content of THE Conversation Workshop and the material on these pages. Our hope is that you not only are inspired to talk differently with the children in your lives about the body, relationships, and sex, but that you feel more equipped to do so.

In the concluding pages of our book, we'd like to highlight the truths we've explored so far, and demonstrate how they weave together to inform your conversations that culminate in "the sex talk." If you are getting ready or planning to present "the talk" with your child or the kids you mentor, we strongly encourage you to start at this beginning of this book and move through the "Conversations" sections of each chapter before using these scripts.

The foundational concepts we have discussed in this book are found below. These concepts are based on the narrative of Scripture in Genesis 1-3, in Jesus's commentary on marriage in Matthew 19:1-12, and in Paul's commentary on marriage in Ephesians 5:31-32, and are also drawn from the themes of the dignity of the human person and marriage that run throughout the Bible. There are over 1,000 verses of Scripture referenced in Pope John Paul II's *Theology of the Body* that have inspired and informed the content in our writings.

## Foundational Concepts

- The body has meaning and dignity. It expresses my person. I cannot separate my body from my person.

- I am a person of beauty and dignity as a creation of God, reflecting who he is. I don't need others to affirm me in order to be okay.

- It is damaging to use my body to take what I want from another person.

- It is damaging to use the bodies of others to take what I want.

- My body cannot be separated from who I am. My actions have an effect on my whole Self—not just my body. I hurt myself if my body-self acts in ways that are contrary to God's design. I experience the best kind of life, the one that God desires for me, when my body-self acts in ways that are consistent with God's design.

- God invites me to be fully satisfied by getting closer to him than my closest friend. I can be just as fully satisfied and happy in life if I get married or if I remain single and celibate.

- When I experience a desire to use another person for my own pleasure, I can choose instead to love and value that person as someone worthy only of God's kind of Love.

- Love does not equal sex. I can love someone fully without giving my body to another person in sexual union.

- When I give myself as a gift to others and the world, I find the best and most joyful kind of life.

### "The Sex Talk" with a Child Who is Not Yet Pre-Adolescent

God created human beings in the very beginning as body-persons. One important thing to know about body-persons is that our bodies speak. Our bodies send messages to others without using words. For example, if I look you in the eyes, smile, and give you a hug, my body speaks a message that I love you.

When God created men and women in the beginning, he planned that they would have a special kind of relationship that is different from all others. He calls this relationship a marriage. A marriage happens when the man and woman speak words that are a promise or vow to each other in front of God and the people who love them. They say this promise to each other and it sounds something like, "I give myself freely, totally, and only to you. I am becoming one with you until our lives are over." And in this marriage relationship, the bodies of the husband and wife also speak very serious promises or vows to one another. They become close in a way that is very special for a husband and wife. Their bodies speak this message: "I give myself freely, totally, and only to you. I am becoming one with you until our lives are over."

This is God's design for (or "the special way that God created") sex.

When we trust God's design for us as human persons, we will have the most joyful and best kind of life, a life that flourishes.

**"The Sex Talk" with Pre-Adolescent Children**

As human persons approach the teenage years, male and female bodies begin to change. God designed us from the very beginning as male and female. The physical changes we go through prepare us for new ways to reflect God's image through our bodies. As we talk about these changes, we'll notice that they're actually clues to God's plan for giving and receiving love in the future.

Male and female bodies are made in such a way that within a marriage relationship they are a picture of God's love-giving and life-giving. When a man and a woman get married, their bodies join in the most intimate way and speak of total love and union with one another in a covenant relationship. This union can remind them of their love and marriage vows that sound something like this: "I give myself totally and only to you until death do us part." This union can also result in the creation of a new life. The very special way our bodies can become life-giving is through the conception of a baby.

This is God's design for sex and marriage and his direction for lives of flourishing.

Marriage is a one-of-a-kind relationship. Even though marriage is the only relationship where two people make vows of total lifelong union with both their words and their bodies, it's God's plan that all of our relationships be both love-giving and life-giving in different ways. In the future, you might feel called to be married or you might feel called to live life as a single person. In either case, you will be challenged to give of yourself unselfishly to another, reflecting God's life-giving and love-giving nature. You can begin to practice loving like God does even now. 1 John 3:16 (NLT) tells us, "We know what real love is because Jesus gave up his life for us. So we also ought to give up our lives for our brothers and sisters." What are some ways that you have unselfishly given of yourself to another person?

## MORE RESOURCES

We sincerely hope that this book has been of help to you in your conversations with the kids in your lives. For further help, we also offer a one-day interactive workshop for parents and mentors and would invite you to learn more about it on our website: theconversationworkshop.com. You may also find our podcasts on the website at theconversationworkshop.com/podcasts.

**Appendix A: The Satisfaction of All My Desires**

The following are Scripture references showing that God alone can satisfy all of our desires and needs, and describe who he longs to be in our lives. These can be used in your conversations with young people.

**Strength/Fulfillment** Ps. 73:25 (NASB) Whom have I in heaven *but You?* And besides You I desire nothing on earth. My flesh and my heart may fail, But God is the strength of my heart and my portion forever.

**A Person to Admire/Be Proud Of** Zeph. 3:17 (NASB) The LORD your God is in your midst, A victorious warrior.

**My Biggest Fan** Zeph. 3:17 (NASB) He will exult over you with joy, He will be quiet in His love, He will rejoice over you with shouts of joy.

**Fun to Be With** Ps. 90:14 (NASB) O satisfy us in the morning with Your lovingkindness, That we may sing for joy and be glad all our days.

**Holds My Hand** Ps. 73:23 (NASB) Nevertheless I am continually with You; You have taken hold of my right hand.

**I Can Lean On Him For Advice on Life's Issues** Ps. 73:23-24 (NASB) Nevertheless I am continually with You...with Your counsel You will guide me.

**Pursues Me** Ps. 23:6 (NLT) Surely your goodness and unfailing love will pursue me all the days of my life...

**Cheers Me Up** Ps. 30:11 (NASB) You have turned for me my mourning into dancing...

**Is With Me and Gives Strength in Difficult Times** Ps. 138:7 (NASB) Though I walk in the midst of trouble, You will revive me...And Your right hand will save me.

**Notices My Needs** Ps. 138:8 (NASB) The Lord will accomplish what concerns me; Your lovingkindness, O LORD, is everlasting.

**Dances With Me** Jeremiah 31:4 (NIV) I will build you up again and you...will be rebuilt. Again you will take up your timbrels and go out to dance with the joyful.

**Supports Me** Psalm 94:18 (NLT) I cried out, "I'm slipping!" but your unfailing love, O LORD, supported me.

**Satisfies My Longings** Ps. 107:9 (NASB) For He has satisfied the thirsty soul, And the hungry soul He has filled with what is good.

**REALLY Satisfies Me** Ps. 63:3 & 5 (NASB) Because Your lovingkindness is better than life, my lips will praise You...My soul is satisfied...

**Defends and Rescues Me** Ps. 54:1 (NLT) Come with great power, O God, and rescue me. Defend me with your might.

**Will Not Abandon Me** Ps. 100:5 (NASB) For the LORD is good; His lovingkindness is everlasting and His faithfulness to all generations.

**Talks With Me/Does Life With Me** Isaiah 30:21 (NASB) Your ears will hear a word behind you, "This is the way, walk in it," whenever you turn to the right or to the left.

**Calms Me When I'm Scared** Deut. 31:6 (NASB) Be strong and courageous, do not be afraid or tremble at them, for the Lord your God is the one who goes with you. He will not fail you or forsake you.

**Laughs With Me** Ps. 126:2 (NASB) Then our mouth was filled with laughter and our tongue with joyful shouting...

**Gives Me Good Gifts** Ps. 84:11-12 (NIV) No good thing does he withhold from those whose walk is blameless. Lord Almighty, blessed is the one who trusts in you.

**Hears Me** Ps. 4:3 (NIV) ...The LORD hears when I call to him.

**Deeply Fills Me** Rom. 8:11 (NASB) But if the Spirit of Him who raised Jesus from the dead dwells in you, He who raised Christ Jesus from the dead will also give life to your mortal bodies through His Spirit who indwells you.

**Gives Me A Secure Future** Jeremiah 29:11 (NIV) "For I know the plans I have for you," declares the Lord, "plans to prosper you and not to harm you, plans to give you a hope and a future."

**Never Forgets or Overlooks Me** Isaiah 49:16 (NASB) Behold, I have inscribed you on the palms of *My hands*.

**Is Close To Me** Ps. 145:18 (NASB) The LORD is near to all who call upon Him...

**Enjoys Me** Ps. 149:4 (NASB) For the LORD takes pleasure in His people...

**Picks Me Up After Failing** Ps. 37:23 (NASB) The steps of a man are established by the LORD and He delights in his way. When he falls, he shall not be hurled headlong because the LORD is the One who holds his hand.

**Can't Take His Eyes Off of Me** Ps. 32:8 (NASB) ...I will counsel you with my eye upon you.

## Appendix B: Teaching Kids What Love *Doesn't* Look Like

Per our discussion in chapter 18, there are times when any one of us, including youth, experience something that falls far short of God's kind of Love. Conversations that help young people to understand what love doesn't look like can serve to help protect them and others from those who intend harm. Here is a little further discussion on this point as well as a suggested script that might be helpful if you want to have this specific conversation with a child you care for.

Remember, our goal as parents and mentors is that our children flourish. To flourish is to experience the abundant and satisfying life found in a life permeated in loving God and others.

Love God + Love Others = FLOURISHING!

The personalistic norm—loving others with God's kind of Love and refusing to use any person for our own purposes—results in a life that flourishes.

> We must never look at someone in terms of what we can get out of them. Many think the opposite of love is hatred. But the opposite of love is *using* people. Using people only to "get stuff" is not love; it is greed. When we do that, we treat a person like a thing. People are more important than things! …*Using* is NOT love.[52]

**Using is not love.**

The personalistic norm offers a distinction that informs our kids how TO love and how NOT to love.

Each of our body-selves images God in a unique and unrepeatable way, and we are to be treated with respect and with an attitude of love. We choose to treat others with Jesus's kind of Love. This kind of Love respects and affirms the image of God in all others. This Love is given freely, not demanded or forced. Love cares about others' feelings. Love doesn't use others to get what we want.

This distinction also gives us a way to communicate to our kids how to know when someone is not loving THEM.

**A conversation you can have with children:**

"It is possible that someone might be disrespectful to you. This person might be someone you know and trust, or they might be a stranger. They might suggest or even try to make you to do something you don't want to do, or you don't feel good or right doing. You might be able to tell that they don't care about you and that they are not loving you with Jesus's Love. Someone might try to use you to get something he or she wants. A clue that can help you to know that this person is dangerous is if they try to touch or ask you to touch the parts of yourself that your bathing suit covers (your private parts). Another clue is if they ask you to touch parts of them that a bathing suit covers (their private parts). It is okay to tell this person "NO!" and run away, even if it is someone you know and are used to being around. No matter who they are, if they are too close, you can push or hit them away hard.

If this ever happens, leave where you are and find an older child or adult you feel comfortable with. You can ask someone to call or text me right away and tell me to come get you. I will not be upset with you at all. You are not in trouble—and nothing bad will happen to you or me. Whether you ran away, yelled, or were too confused or afraid to know what to do, you did absolutely nothing wrong. I am not afraid of anyone who tries to hurt you. God and I will handle it."

# Endnotes

1 Christopher West, *Our Bodies Tell God's Story: Discovering the Divine Plan for Love, Sex, and Gender* (Grand Rapids, MI: BrazosPress, 2019), XV.

2 Matthew Anderson, "God Has a Wonderful Plan for Your Body." *Christianity Today.* August 2011, https://www.christianitytoday.com/ct/2011/august/godhasplanforbody.html

3 Ann Voskamp, *Unwrapping the Greatest Gift: A Family Celebration of Christmas* (Carol Stream, IL: Tyndale House Publishers, Inc., 2014).

4 "Flourishing." *Wikipedia.* https://en.wikipedia.org/wiki/Flourishing (last modified January 9, 2021).

5 Irenaeus, *Against Heresies* (85AD, *Against Heresies* (Lib. 4, 20, 5-7; SC 100, 640-642, 644-648, 185AD). This reading appears in the Roman Office of Readings on the feast (liturgical memorial) of Saint Irenaeus on June 28.

6 C.S. Lewis, *Mere Christianity* (San Francisco: HarperOne, 2015).

7 Karol Wojtyla, *Love and Responsibility* (San Francisco: Ignatius Press, 1993), 41.

8 C.S. Lewis, *The Weight of Glory and Other Addresses* (New York: Touchstone, 1975), 39.

9 James Michael Sama, "What Love Does (And Doesn't) Look Like." *Huffington Post.* December 3, 2013. https://tinyurl.com/y6q8sftx

10 "Love." Google Dictionary. https://www.google.com/search?q=google+dictionary+english+to+english&oq=google+-dictionary&aqs=chrome.2.69i57j0l7.7175j0j4&sourceid=-chrome&ie=UTF-8&safe=active&ssui=on#dobs=love (accessed January 21, 2021).

11 "Children, Teens, Media, and Body Image." *Common Sense Media.* January 21, 2015. https://www.commonsensemedia.org/research/children-teens-media-and-body-image.cam-body-image-report-012615-interactive.pdf, 15.

12 Catholic Church, *Catechism of the Catholic Church*, 2nd ed. (Vatican: Libreria Editrice Vaticana, 2012), paragraph 221.

13 Pope John Paul II, *Theology of the Body*, 19:4.

14 Max Lucado, *If I Only Had a Green Nose* (Wheaton, IL: Crossway Books, 2002).

15 Dr. Dan Allender, "Shame-faced." *Allender Center at the Seattle School.* February 14, 2018. https://theallendercenter.org/2018/02/shame-faced/

16 Allender, "Shame-faced."

17 Christopher West, *Theology of the Body for Beginners* (West Chester, PA: Ascension Press, 2004), 25.

18 West, *Theology of the Body for Beginners*, 69.

19 C.S. Lewis, *The Great Divorce, Revised Edition* (San Francisco: HarperOne, 2015).

20 Lewis, *The Great Divorce*.

21 Belinda Luscombe, "Who Needs Marriage? A Changing Institution." *Time.* November 18, 2010. http://content.time.com/time/magazine/article/0,9171,2032116,00.html

22 Luscombe, "Who Needs Marriage?"

23 Lauren Fox, "The Science of Cohabitation: A Step Toward Marriage, Not a Rebellion." *The Atlantic.* March 20, 2014. https://www.theatlantic.com/health/archive/2014/03/the-science-of-cohabitation-a-step-toward-marriage-not-a-rebellion/284512/

24 Samantha Cooney, "Why People Are So Obsessed with *The Bachelor*, According to the Woman Who Wrote a Book About It." *Time.* March 4, 2018. https://time.com/5168186/bachelor-book-interview/

25 Cooney, "Why People Are So Obsessed with *The Bachelor*."

26 CNN, "For 'Bachelor' viewers, the 'absurdity' is the fun." *GANT News.* March 15, 2017. https://gantdaily.com/2017/03/14/for-bachelor-viewers-the-absurdity-is-the-fun/

27 "20 Mind-Blowing Stats About The Porn Industry And Its Underage Consumers." *Fight the New Drug.* December 4, 2020. https://fightthenewdrug.org/10-porn-stats-that-will-blow-your-mind/

28 Ernest Becker, *The Denial of Death* (New York: Free Press, 1997).

29 "apocalyptic." *Merriam-Webster.com.* 2021. https://www.merriam-webster.com/dictionary/apocalyptic (accessed January 22, 2021).

30 Lewis, *The Weight of Glory.*

31 David Mathis, "We Are Far Too Easily Pleased." *Desiring God.* May 23, 2013. https://www.desiringgod.org/articles/we-are-far-too-easily-pleased

32 Lewis, *The Weight of Glory.*

33 Maggie Seaver, "This is How Much a Wedding Costs on Average, According to Real Data." *The Knot.* https://www.theknot.com/content/average-wedding-cost (accessed January 22, 2021).

34 Esther Lee, "The Top Wedding Trends of 2021." *The Knot.* https://www.theknot.com/content/new-wedding-trends (accessed January 22, 2021).

35 "covenant." *Bible Study Tools.* https://www.biblestudytools.com/dictionary/covenant/ (accessed January 22, 2021).

36 James Orr, "Covenant, In the Old Testament." *Bible Study Tools.* https://www.biblestudytools.com/encyclopedias/isbe/covenant-in-the-old-testament.html (accessed January 22, 2021).

37 "marriage, between God and his people." *Bible Gateway.* https://www.biblegateway.com/resources/dictionary-of-bible-themes/5712-marriage-between-God-his (accessed January 22, 2021).

38 West, *Our Bodies Tell God's Story*, 118.

39 Lauren Winner, "Solitary Refinement." *Christianity Today.* June 11, 2001. https://www.christianitytoday.com/ct/2001/june11/1.30.html

40 Jeremy Erickson, "Protestant Opposition to Celibacy." *Spiritual Friendship: Musings on God, Sexuality, Friendships.* https://spiritualfriendship.org/2015/11/24/protestant-opposition-to-celibacy/ (accessed January 22, 2021).

41 Susan Mobley, Ph.D., "The Reformation and the Reform of Marriage: Historical Views and Background for Today's Disputes." *Issues in Christian Education.* https://issues.cune.edu/the-lgbt-disputes-teaching-and-practice-in-the-church-2/the-reformation-and-the-reform-of-marriage-historical-views-and-background-for-todays-dis-

putes/ (accessed January 22, 2021).

42 Erickson, "Protestant Opposition to Celibacy."

43 Katelyn Beaty, "Same-Sex Marriage and the Single Christian." *Christianity Today.* July 1, 2013. https://www.christianitytoday.com/ct/2013/july-web-only/same-sex-marriage-and-single-christian.html

44 Brother Lawrence, "The Practice of the Presence of God" (London: The Epworth Press). https://d2y1pz2y630308.cloudfront.net/15471/documents/2016/10/Brother%20Lawrence-The%20Practice%20of%20the%20Presence%20of%20God.pdf.

45 Christopher West, "The Theology of the Body: An Education in Being Human." *University of Notre Dame.* https://www3.nd.edu/~afreddos/courses/264/west2.htm

46 Karol Wojtyla, *Love and Responsibility* (San Francisco: Ignatius Press, 1993), 41.

47 Wojtyla, *Love and Responsibility.*

48 Lewis, *Mere Christianity.*

49 Christopher West, *Theology of the Body Explained* (Boston, MA: Pauline Books and Media, 2003).

50 "Personalistic Norm," *Theology of the Body,* 26-27.

51 Lewis, *Mere Christianity.*

52 The Body Matters Team, "The Body as a Sacrament." *The Body Matters A Theology of the Body Curriculum* (TOBET Press, 2017). https://tobet.org/wp-content/uploads/woocommerce_uploads/2017/10/TO-BET-The-Body-as-Sacrament-Educator-Guide.pdf

# About the Authors

Linda Noble, the Ministry Director at Journey Community Church in La Mesa, California, has conducted multiple classes, workshops, and seminars introducing *Theology of the Body*. Linda is the mother of three adult children, all of whom serve with her and her husband at Journey. She has been working at the church for twenty years writing curriculum, speaking and teaching, facilitating small groups, and mentoring. *Sacred Life Curriculum*, written by Linda for children K-12 in faith-based schools, has been published by an arm of Nazarene Publishing.

Linda Stewart is a Licensed Marriage and Family Therapist and Supervisor at the Safe Haven Relationship Center in Carlsbad, California. She introduces a *Theology of the Body* based approach and model when training other clinicians and lay counselors. Linda has been a speaker, trainer, and facilitator for youth and church groups for twenty years. She is married with two daughters.

The Lindas began facilitating THE Conversation Workshop in 2017 after months of working to create and facilitate five accessible, challenging, and interactive sessions for parents and mentors. This workshop can give you the resources you need to help you talk with kids about God's design for the body, relationships, and sex. Find a workshop, get info on hosting a workshop, and discover more resources on our website: www.theconversationworkshop. com. There you can also listen to podcasts as we share portions of our workshop content, get answers to your questions on our Q&A page, and download helpful pages full of conversation starters. THE Conversation Workshop became a 501(c)(3) nonprofit in 2019.

Made in the USA
Monee, IL
08 September 2024

65219214R00085